# Mediterranean Diet Cookbook

*1500 Days of Easy & Affordable Recipes for Beginners | 15-Week Simple & Flexible Meal Plan to Kickstart Your New Life*

## By Victoria Douglas

© **Copyright 2022 - All rights reserved.**

The content contained within this book may not be reproduced, duplicated, or transmitted without direct written permission from the author or the publisher.

Under no circumstances will any blame or legal responsibility be held against the publisher, or author, for any damages, reparation, or monetary loss due to the information contained within this book. Either directly or indirectly.

**Legal Notice:**

This book is copyright protected. This book is only for personal use. You cannot amend, distribute, sell, use, quote or paraphrase any part, or the content within this book, without the consent of the author or publisher.

**Disclaimer Notice:**

Please note the information contained within this document is for educational and entertainment purposes only. All effort has been executed to present accurate, up to date, and reliable, complete information. No warranties of any kind are declared or implied. Readers acknowledge that the author is not engaging in the rendering of legal, financial, medical or professional advice. The content within this book has been derived from various sources. Please consult a licensed professional before attempting any techniques outlined in this book.

By reading this document, the reader agrees that under no circumstances is the author responsible for any losses, direct or indirect, which are incurred because of the use of information contained within this document, including, but not limited to, — errors, omissions, or inaccuracies.

# Table of Contents

INTRODUCTION ... 4

HOW TO BUILD THE HEALTHIEST MEDITERRANEAN HABITS ... 5

THE MEDITERRANEAN DIET FOOD SHOPPING LIST ... 6

MEDITERRANEAN COOKING TECHNIQUES ... 7

3 BENEFITS OF THE MEDITERRANEAN DIET ... 7

MEAL PLAN ... 8

MEDITERRANEAN DIET RECIPES ... 15

BREAKFAST BRUNCH AND SMOOTHIES ... 16

APPETIZERS, DIPS AND SNACKS ... 28

SALADS AND WARM VEGGIES ... 37

STEW AND SOUP RECIPES ... 47

BEANS, RICE, AND GRAINS ... 59

MAINS ... 67

KIDS FRIENDLY RECIPES ... 76

FRUITS, SWEETS, AND DESSERTS ... 80

CONVERSION CHARTS ... 88

RECIPES INDEX ... 89

FINAL WORDS ... 91

THANK YOU ... 92

# Introduction

The term "diet" for most of us spells out deprivation, extreme hunger, and bland and boring foods that we are forced to eat in order to lose weight. However, with the Mediterranean diet, none of those apply.

The Mediterranean diet is endowed with an unlimited assortment of fresh, healthy, natural, and wholesome foods from all food groups. Although there is a greater focus on certain components, no natural components are excluded.

Mediterranean diet devotees can enjoy their favorite dishes as they learn to appreciate how nourishing the freshest healthy and natural foods can be.

This diet is primarily based on the eating habits of the original inhabitants of the coasts of Greece, Italy, Spain, Morocco, and France. Because of their temperate climate and location, seasonal fruit, vegetables, and seafood are from these regions' nutritional foundations.

The easiest way to understand the Mediterranean diet is to picture eating as though it's summer every day. It might also give you a déjà vu moment by reminding you of the foods you enjoyed most on a summer vacation or at the beach. In truth, there is never a dull moment with the Mediterranean diet! All fun aside, the Mediterranean diet will help you find great pleasure in food, knowing that every bite you take will provide your body with the healthiest nutrition.

When your food tastes like you are on a perpetual vacation, it's easy ad exciting to stay on the bandwagon!

Invest in minimally processed foods that promote the Mediterranean Diet, the healthiest dietary pattern. The Mediterranean way of eating is centuries old; however, it has only recently become the subject of scientific nutrition research.

There is an abundance of evidence that shows eating whole grains, healthy fats, and lean proteins coupled with moderate amounts of wine can extend the life and stave off chronic diseases like heart disease and diabetes. Specifically, researchers found that following a Mediterranean diet over five years resulted in a 30% lower incidence of heart attacks, strokes, and deaths from heart disease among high-risk individuals compared to those eating a low-fat diet.

Mediterranean diets emphasize foods that can prevent inflammation and oxidative stress, which contribute to many chronic ailments. Fish rich in omega-3 fatty acids, fruits, vegetables, nuts and seeds, and healthy oils are some of these foods. Dietary patterns using monounsaturated fats are especially beneficial to the cardiovascular system as they lower bad LDL cholesterol and raise good HDL cholesterol. Moreover, a large proportion of foods that are plant-based are rich in fiber and phytonutrients.

Mediterranean diets emphasize plant foods over processed foods, added sugar, and saturated fat. Red meat, sweets, and full-fat dairy are consumed occasionally, although full-fat dairy is still consumed in moderation. Occasionally, wine is consumed with dinner, but water is preferred when it's not poured.

The Mediterranean lifestyle goes beyond specific food groups to emphasize healthy habits such as cooking at home (and enjoying it with friends and family), living an active lifestyle, and adopting mindful eating habits.

In essence, the Mediterranean diet involves quite a simple culinary landscape. Essentially, it relies on preparing fresh, seasonal ingredients to let each ingredient's quality and natural taste stand out.

# How To Build the Healthiest Mediterranean Habits

You can follow these steps to move toward a more Mediterranean-style diet. Choose one of the suggestions below, and practice it. Next, try one of the other suggestions. These eight tips for making over your plate will help you reap the health benefits of a Mediterranean diet, no matter where you begin.

### 1. Cook with Olive Oil
Consider replacing coconut oil or vegetable oil with extra-virgin olive oil if you currently cook with them. This "good" type of cholesterol may be improved by monounsaturated fats found in olive oil. According to a 2017 study published in Circulation, HDL cholesterol transports "bad" LDL particles out of arteries. Dress salads and go with homemade vinaigrettes using olive oil. Use it to enhance the flavor of finished dishes such as chicken and fish. You can substitute olive oil for butter in mashed potatoes and pasta.

### 2. Eat More Fish
Fish is the main source of protein in the Mediterranean diet. Salmon, sardines, and mackerel are especially used in this diet. Healthy omega-3 fatty acids are abundant in these fish. The low-fat fish (such as cod or tilapia) provide good protein, so even the leaner ones are still worth it. An easy way to get more fish into your diet if you don't currently get a lot of fish is to designate one night a week as fish night. A no-fuss, no-mess method of cooking fish is to place it in parchment or foil packets before cooking. Or try incorporating it into your favorite food, such as tacos, soups, and stir-fries.

### 3. Eat Veggies All Day Long
It's a perfect time to add a few more veggies to your diet if you worry you don't eat enough greens. If you want to eat two servings each, you can try munching on bell pepper strips at snack time or adding a handful of spinach to a smoothie at dinner time, like these easy and quick sides. Every day, you should consume two servings. A larger serving is better. Australian research notes that you should consume three servings every day to alleviate stress.

### 4. Help Yourself to Whole Grains
Test "real" whole grains that haven't been refined and are still "whole." It takes just 20 minutes to cook Quinoa, making it an easy side dish for busy weeknights. A steaming bowl of mushroom soup with barley will leave you feeling full and satisfied. Barley is filled with fiber and is filling. When the weather is cold, oatmeal makes the perfect breakfast.

If you eat popcorn, make sure it's air-popped and forgo the butter (use olive oil instead). Other whole-grain products like whole-wheat pasta and bread can complement your intake. On the food package and in the ingredient list, look for the term "whole" or "whole grain"-it should appear as the first ingredient. To make the switch from refined to whole grains, you can use whole-grain blends of pasta and rice or mix a whole grain with a refined one (like half whole-wheat pasta, half white pasta).

### 5. Snack on Nuts
Mediterranean diets also include nuts. If you want a snack that will keep you satisfied, grab a handful of almonds, cashews, or pistachios. In a study published in Nutrition Journal, people who replace their standard snack with almonds will consume fewer empty calories, added sugars, and sodium. The vitamins and minerals in nuts, such as potassium, are higher than those in processed snacks.

### 6. Enjoy fruit for Dessert
Fresh fruit is a healthy way to indulge your sweet tooth because it is a good source of fiber, vitamin C, and antioxidants. Sprinkle a little brown sugar on grapefruit or drizzle slices of pear with honey if it encourages you to eat more. Fresh fruit should be visible at home, and you should keep one or two at work for when you feel hungry. Pick up a new exotic fruit each week from your local grocery store and expand your fruit palate.

### 7. Sip (a Little) Wine
Spaniards, Italians, French, Greeks, and others who live along the Mediterranean do not shy away from wine, but that doesn't mean you should pour it at your leisure. For the New England Journal of Medicine study, the dietitians and experts who developed the Mediterranean diet recommended women consume 3 ounces of fish per day and men 5 ounces. If you decide to sip, try to do so with a meal, especially if it is a meal shared with loved ones. It won't do any good to start drinking for this diet if you're teetotal.

# The Mediterranean Diet Food Shopping List

### Extra-virgin olive oil
Although olive oil plays an important role in each Mediterranean diet, the overall Mediterranean diet has a variety of dietary patterns. Its antioxidant and anti-inflammatory properties are attributed to its rich content of tocopherols, carotenoids, and polyphenols. As versatile in the kitchen, as it is in everyday staples such as dips, spreads, and dressings, this pantry staple is ideal for cooking and eating. To ensure you're getting high-quality olive oil, look for a bottle in a dark color. Fats become rancid when exposed to light and heat, and tinting protects them. Keep the oil cool and dark once you get it home in order to preserve its quality.

### Fresh fruits and veggies
Traditionally, Mediterranean cuisine emphasizes fresh, local, seasonal ingredients. Frittatas, beans, and lentil soups often contain dark leafy greens such as collard greens, beet greens, and mustard greens. Both raw and cooked recipes use wild greens like chicory, rocket, and dandelion. Besides artichokes and beets, this region produces broccoli, cucumber, eggplant, mushrooms, radishes, and onions. A mainstay in Mediterranean cuisine is garlic.

### Fresh herbs and spices
In Mediterranean cooking, spices and herbs play an important role. Seasonings derived from plants can reduce the need for salting food excessively as well as provide antioxidants that are health-promoting. You will frequently find bay leaves, parsley, basil, oregano, and oregano in the Mediterranean.

### Fresh and canned seafood
Among the key ingredients of the Mediterranean diet are fish and shellfish. Fish such as tuna, salmon, and sardines, which are rich in omega-3 fatty acids, are available fresh or canned. The seafood of the sea is commonly found in pasta dishes and grain dishes or simply served with lemon, olive oil, and herbs. Seafood consumption is common in Mediterranean cultures.

### Whole grains
The Mediterranean diet is based on wheat. Traditional Italian dishes and salads use farro as a grain. As well as bulgur, another classic grain, is tabbouleh, which is made from cracked wheatberries. Aside from rice, pasta, and barley, couscous and pasta are also popular in many regions. The term "whole grain" and "whole grain" should appear on the package and on the ingredient list of whole grains.

### Legumes (dried and canned)
Mediterranean cuisine uses chickpeas often for hummus, falafel, and salad dressings. The fiber and protein in lentils make them an excellent addition to soups and stews. A drizzle of olive oil and a fresh squeeze of lemon is commonly used to dress salads in black-eyed peas, kidney beans, and cannellini beans.

### Nuts and seeds
Fiber, protein, and fat all combine to make nuts and seeds a satisfying snack. Tahini is a condiment common along the Mediterranean coast that is made from ground sesame seeds. Hummus is most famous for using this versatile condiment, but it is also an excellent topping for salad dressings. For roasted vegetables or grain bowls, use them in sauces or dressings.

### Olives and capers
Olives are enjoyed as a simple snack or as a complement to crudites. Kalamata olives are among the most popular and are commonly used as an ingredient in salads and pasta in Greece. Omega-3 fatty acids and antioxidant polyphenols are abundant in olives. Whether they are brined or dried, capers contribute a tasteful twist to pasta, baked fish, and salad dressings.

### Canned tomatoes
Both canned and fresh tomatoes are staples in the Mediterranean region, whether they are whole, diced, stewed, or concentrated into a paste. In canned tomatoes, lycopene content is high (due to the heating process), which may help protect against certain cancers. Toasted fish with tomatoes, stuffed tomatoes, shakshuka, and marinara sauce are some tomato-centric traditions from the Mediterranean.

### Greek yogurt and artisanal cheeses
The Mediterranean diet encourages the consumption of fruits, vegetables, and whole grains, as well as small amounts of full-fat dairy. Fermented yogurt is rich in gut-healthy probiotics as well as additional protein for plant-centric meals. Unlike the more processed cheeses available in the U.S., this region specializes in cultured cheeses (made with milk and natural cultures).
Feta cheese is often served with stews or fish dishes as well as in the classic Greek salad. Grilling and frying are both effective methods to prepare Halloumi cheese because of its firm texture. In egg dishes, harder cheeses such as Pecorino Romano and Parmigiano-Reggiano are sometimes grated into pasta. Manchego can be baked into pasta.

# Mediterranean Cooking Techniques

### Battuto
- Start making either battuto, as it is known in Italian, or sofrito, as it is called in Spanish, if you're not sure how to get started. French cooking uses a mirepoix, which contains carrots, celery, and onion chopped and cooked with olive oil, garlic, and herbs. As a base for pasta sauces, soups, stews, or to marinate beans, you can use this.

### Soaking Beans
- It is traditional in Mediterranean cooking to soak beans and all legumes prior to cooking. In addition to speeding up the cooking process, soaking beans may also ease digestion. You can soak them either quickly or overnight.
- Quick-soaking beans are covered with boiling water, then soaked at room temperature for an hour before cooking.
- In either case, soaking for 8-12 hours in room temperature water will work well. For cooking, you must discard the soaking water and add fresh water.
- Cooked beans should be seasoned with salt after they are cooked. Cooking beans in the broth will also enhance their flavor

### Take Things Slow
- We live in a culture that is far more fast-paced in the USA than in Europe. You can slow down your home cooking by adding a few of these Mediterranean tips. Plan your meals ahead of time and have a relaxing time cooking.

# 3 Benefits Of The Mediterranean Diet

If we take an in-depth look at the Mediterranean diet, it's not a *diet* per se as a weight-loss tool—it's more of a lifestyle and a culinary tradition for the people of the Mediterranean region. Its primary focus is on whole grains, fruit and vegetables, seafood, nuts, olive oil, and a glass of wine now and then. This diet is part of a culture that appreciates the freshest components, is prepared in a simple but tasty way, and is shared with friends and family in a laid-back environment.

- Most of us understand the vitality of eating a clean and well-balanced diet for improved health and better quality of life, but very few of us place this into practice. With most of us spending a greater percentage of our days at work, we tend to opt for fast and easy options for the food we eat. In fact, in many cases, fast food, frozen dinners from food stores, and processed foods are our first options.
- Over the years, people have stopped eating seasonal worldwide foods because we can now access all kinds of food all year round. What's more, cooking meals from scratch seems to be an unnecessary hassle, considering our overburdened schedules & the time it requires to make a good meal. As a result, we are eating foods that are made from a plant instead of food that grows like a plant. Our diets are characterized by over-processed foods, unhealthy fats, truckloads of sugar, and lots and lots of artificial ingredients, the names of which most of us can't even pronounce.
- Perhaps one of the greatest attributes of the Mediterranean diet is the fact that it is very simple and direct. You have not to be an expert to make the meals, as you will learn in our recipes section. Eat less red meat and more fish—especially fatty fish rich in omega-3 fatty acids—cook with olive oil, and eat fruit, vegetables, whole grains, and nuts several times a day.
- Unlike many popular diets, many of which are fads, the Mediterranean diet encourages healthy fats from olive oil, nuts, seeds, fish, and avocado. Sometimes, the occasional glass of red wine lowers your risk of heart disease.

# Meal Plan

| | Breakfast & Brunch Recipes | Lunch Recipes | Dinner recipes | Snacks & Appetizer Recipes | Dessert Recipes |
|---|---|---|---|---|---|
| Day 1 | Egg, Pancetta, and Spinach Benedict .. 8, 10, 17 | Cauliflower Tabbouleh 8, 10, 18 | Braised Chicken with Mushrooms and Olives 9, 12, 18 | Guaca Egg Scramble 8, 10, 18 | Banana Shake Bowls 8, 9, 10, 11, 12, 13, 14, 28 |
| Day 2 | Avocado Toast 25 | Bagna Cauda 9, 10, 11, 13, 18 | Turkey and Asparagus Mix 8, 9, 10, 11, 12, 13, 26, 18, 19, 20, 21, 22 | Garlicky Scrambled Eggs 26 | Creamy Mint Strawberry Mix 8, 10, 12, 34 |
| Day 3 | Freekeh Pilaf 3, 9, 10, 11, 13, 14, 18 | Baked Black-Eyed Peas 10, 11, 13, 14, 18 | Asparagus Avocado Soup 11, 12, 23 | Avocado Toast 25 | Blueberries Stew 8, 10, 12, 33 |
| Day 4 | Breakfast Couscous 8, 9, 11, 12, 13, 14, 19, 23, 25 | Baked Ricotta & Pears 12, 18 | Brown Rice Pilaf with Raisins 11, 13, 18 | Belizean Chicken Stew 13, 22 | Rhubarb and Apple Cream 9, 11, 12, 32m |
| Day 5 | Eggs and Greens 8, 11, 18 | Banana Cinnamon Cupcakes 9, 11, 13, 31 | Cheesy Stuffed Tomatoes 10, 11, 13, 14, 19 | Garlic and Lemon Chicken Dish 21 | Cardamom Almond Cream 9, 11, 13, 31 |
| Day 6 | Fava Beans With Basmati Rice 10, 11, 18 | Battuto 7 | Chicken and Leeks Pan 12, 19 | Chicken and Peppers Mix 12, 20 | Cinnamon Chickpeas Cookies 9, 10, 11, 13, 30 |
| Day 7 | Fermented yogurt 6 | Bulgur Salad with Carrots and Almonds 8, 9, 10, 11, 12, 14, 18, 22 | Chicken and Peppers Mix 12, 20 | Chicken and Leeks Pan 12, 19 | Black Tea Cake 9, 10, 11, 14, 29 |
| Day 8 | Freekeh Pilaf 3, 9, 10, 11, 13, 14, 18 | Cauliflower Soup 8, 11, 12, 22 | Chicken Shawarma 9, 10, 18 | Cannellini Bean Soup 20 | Banana Shake Bowls 8, 9, 10, 11, 12, 13, 14, 28 |
| Day 9 | Fresh Tomato Pasta Bowl 8, 11, 12, 18 | Cauliflower Tabbouleh 8, 10, 18 | Chicken Skillet 9, 11, 12, 13, 18 | Garlicky Broiled Sardines 11, 12, 18 | Almond Rice Dessert 9, 11, 12, 32 |
| Day 10 | Full Eggs in a Squash 8, 11, 12, 18 | Cauliflower and Cherry Tomato Salad 10, 11, 18 | Chicken Stuffed Peppers 8, 12, 18 | Garlic and Lemon Chicken Dish 21 | Arugula and Mango 8, 9, 10, 14, 18 |
| Day 11 | Citrus-Kissed Melon 12, 18 | Carrot Salad 8, 10, 18 | Chicken with Greek 8, 11, 18 | Cannellini Beans and Farro Stew 10, 14, 18 | Banana Shake Bowls 8, 9, 10, 11, 12, 13, 14, 28 |
| Day 12 | Garlicky Scrambled Eggs 26 | Citrus Salad 8, 12, 18 | Chicken with Olives, Mustard Greens, and Lemon 11, 18 | Carrot and Bean Stuffed Peppers 8, 9, 14, 18 | CaFE Cooler 8, 10, 18 |

| | | | | | |
|---|---|---|---|---|---|
| Day 13 | Fava Beans With Basmati Rice 10, 11, 18 | Cocoa Brownies 9, 10, 11, 13, 30 | Chickpeas, Tomato and Kale Stew 13, 25 | Chilled Pea and mint soup 19 | Cardamom Almond Cream 9, 11, 13, 31 |
| Day 14 | Freekeh Pilaf 3, 9, 10, 11, 13, 14, 18 | Coronation Chicken Salad Sirtfood 8, 12, 18 | Cold Lemon Squares 8, 9, 10, 11, 12, 13, 14, 28 | Cinnamon Chickpeas Cookies 9, 10, 11, 13, 30 | Banana Shake Bowls 8, 9, 10, 11, 12, 13, 14, 28 |
| Day 15 | Egg, Pancetta, and Spinach Benedict 8, 10, 17 | Cauliflower Tabbouleh 8, 10, 18 | Gnocchi Ham Olives 8, 11, 18 | Coriander Falafel 8, 9, 10, 11, 12, 13, 18, 25, 18 | Creamy Mint Strawberry Mix 8, 10, 12, 34 |
| Day 16 | Avocado Toast 25 | Cauliflower and Cherry Tomato Salad 10, 11, 18 | Greek Inspired Rice 10, 12, 18 | Cold Lemon Squares 8, 9, 10, 11, 12, 13, 14, 28 | Blueberries Stew 8, 10, 12, 33 |
| Day 17 | Freekeh Pilaf 3, 9, 10, 11, 13, 14, 18 | Carrot Salad 8, 10, 18 | Chicken with Greek 8, 11, 18 | Cream of Thyme Tomato Soup 19 | Rhubarb and Apple Cream 9, 11, 12, 32m |
| Day 18 | Breakfast Couscous 8, 9, 11, 12, 13, 14, 19, 23, 25 | Citrus Salad 8, 12, 18 | Chicken with Olives, Mustard Greens, and Lemon 11, 18 | Creamy Cauliflower Soup 8, 9, 10, 12, 21, 34 | Cardamom Almond Cream 9, 11, 13, 31 |
| Day 19 | Eggs and Greens 8, 11, 18 | Cocoa Brownies 9, 10, 11, 13, 30 | Chickpeas, Tomato and Kale Stew 13, 25 | Creamy broccoli soup 8, 9, 10, 11, 13, 18 | Cinnamon Chickpeas Cookies 9, 10, 11, 13, 30 |
| Day 20 | Fava Beans With Basmati Rice 10, 11, 18 | Coronation Chicken Salad Sirtfood 8, 12, 18 | Cold Lemon Squares 8, 9, 10, 11, 12, 13, 14, 28 | Creamy Chicken Soup 11, 13, 26 | Black Tea Cake 9, 10, 11, 14, 29 |
| Day 21 | Fermented yogurt 6 | Cauliflower Tabbouleh 8, 10, 18 | Gnocchi Ham Olives 8, 11, 18 | Creamy Mint Strawberry Mix 8, 10, 12, 34 | Banana Shake Bowls 8, 9, 10, 11, 12, 13, 14, 28 |
| Day 22 | Freekeh Pilaf 3, 9, 10, 11, 13, 14, 18 | Cauliflower and Cherry Tomato Salad 10, 11, 18 | Greek Inspired Rice 10, 12, 18 | Cucumber Soup 11, 13, 14, 24 | Almond Rice Dessert 9, 11, 12, 32 |
| Day 23 | Fresh Tomato Pasta Bowl 8, 11, 12, 18 | Carrot Salad 8, 10, 18 | Ricotta Stuffed Bell Peppers 12, 18 | Rice and Veggie Jambalaya 3, 9, 10, 11, 12, 13, 18 | Dandelion and Strawberry 10, 11, 18 |
| Day 24 | Roasted Asparagus and Tomatoes 12, 18 | Citrus Salad 8, 12, 18 | Mint avocado chilled soup | Ricotta Stuffed Bell Peppers 12, 18 | Banana Shake Bowls 8, 9, 10, 11, 12, 13, 14, 28 |
| Day 25 | Roasted Acorn Squash with Sage 13, 18 | Cocoa Brownies 9, 10, 11, 13, 30 | Pineapple Salsa 8, 11, 12, 18 | Mushroom soup 10, 14, 20, 18 | Creamy Mint Strawberry Mix 8, 10, 12, 34 |
| Day 26 | Rocket Tomatoes and Mushroom Frittata 8, 11, 12, 18 | Polyphenols 6 | Pepper Tapenade 8, 9, 10, 11, 12, 13, 14, 18 | Mushroom barley soup 8, 9, 12, 18 | Blueberries Stew 8, 10, 12, 33 |
| Day 27 | Mediterranean Spiced Lentils 10, 11, 18 | Mediterranean Spinach and Beans 8, 9, 10, 12, 14, 18, 20, 18 | Paprika Chicken Mix 12, 19 | Minty Lentil and Spinach Soup 8, 9, | Rhubarb and Apple Cream 9, 11, 12, 32m |

| | | | | 10, 11, 12, 13, 14, 23 | |
|---|---|---|---|---|---|
| Day 28 | Fava Beans With Basmati Rice 10, 11, 18 | Quinoa, Bean, and Vegetable Stew 12, 18 | Olives and Cheese Stuffed Tomatoes 9, 11, 12, 18 | Mint avocado chilled soup 9, 12, 21 | Peach Sunrise Smoothie 10, 12, 18 |
| Day 29 | Potato And Chickpea Hash 24 | Octopus and Radish Salad 8, 12, 18 | Braised Cauliflower with White Wine | Ratatouille 8, 9, 10, 13, 17, 18 | Rhubarb and Apple Cream 9, 11, 12, 32 |
| Day 30 | Guaca Egg Scramble 8, 10, 18 | Lemon Green Beans with Red Onion 9, 13, 18 | Rice and Veggie Jambalaya 3, 9, 10, 11, 12, 13, 18 | Ricotta Stuffed Bell Peppers 12, 18 | Arugula and Mango 8, 9, 10, 14, 18 |
| Day 31 | Mediterranean Frittata 12, 13, 14, 26 | Heart-Healthful Trail Mix 8, 10, 18 | Braised Chicken with Mushrooms and Olives 9, 12, 18 | Easy Tzatziki Sauce | Banana Shake Bowls 8, 9, 10, 11, 12, 13, 14, 28 |
| Day 32 | Herbed Rice 11, 12, 18 | Cannellini Beans and Farro Stew | Turkey and Asparagus Mix 8, 9, 10, 11, 12, 13, 26, 18, 19, 20, 21, 22 | Green breakfast soup 10, 18 | CaFE Cooler 8, 10, 18 |
| Day 33 | Mediterranean Eggs 13, 18 | Lemon Green Beans with Red Onion 9, 13, 18 | Asparagus Avocado Soup 11, 12, 23 | Honey Balsamic Chicken 8, 9, 12, 20 | Cardamom Almond Cream 9, 11, 13, 31 |
| Day 34 | Avocado Toast 25 | Mandarin Cream 8, 10, 12, 33 | Brown Rice Pilaf with Raisins 11, 13, 18 | Herbed Risotto 8, 10, 19 | Banana Shake Bowls 8, 9, 10, 11, 12, 13, 14, 28 |
| Day 35 | Mediterranean Feta and Quinoa Egg Muffins 1, 3, 4, 5, 6, 7, 9, 10, 11, 12, 13, 15, 18, 37 | Bulgur Salad with Carrots and Almonds 8, 9, 10, 11, 12, 14, 18, 22 | Cheesy Stuffed Tomatoes 10, 11, 13, 14, 19 | Guaca Egg Scramble 8, 10, 18 | Creamy Mint Strawberry Mix 8, 10, 12, 34 |
| Day 36 | Egg, Pancetta, and Spinach Benedict 8, 10, 17 | Bagna Cauda 9, 10, 11, 13, 18 | Chicken and Leeks Pan 12, 19 | Garlicky Scrambled Eggs 26 | Blueberries Stew 8, 10, 12, 33 |
| Day 37 | Avocado Toast 25 | Baked Black-Eyed Peas 10, 11, 13, 14, 18 | Chicken and Peppers Mix 12, 20 | Avocado Toast 25 | Rhubarb and Apple Cream 9, 11, 12, 32m |
| Day 38 | Freekeh Pilaf 3, 9, 10, 11, 13, 14, 18 | Baked Ricotta & Pears 12, 18 | Chicken Shawarma 9, 10, 18 | Belizean Chicken Stew 13, 22 | Cardamom Almond Cream 9, 11, 13, 31 |
| Day 39 | Breakfast Couscous 8, 9, 11, 12, 13, 14, 19, 23, 25 | Banana Cinnamon Cupcakes 9, 11, 13, 31 | Chicken Skillet 9, 11, 12, 13, 18 | Garlic and Lemon Chicken Dish 21 | Cinnamon Chickpeas Cookies 9, 10, 11, 13, 30 |
| Day 40 | Eggs and Greens 8, 11, 18 | Battuto 7 | Chicken Stuffed Peppers 8, 12, 18 | Chicken and Peppers Mix 12, 20 | Black Tea Cake 9, 10, 11, 14, 29 |
| Day 41 | Fava Beans With Basmati Rice 10, 11, 18 | Bulgur Salad with Carrots and | Chicken with Greek 8, 11, 18 | Chicken and Leeks Pan 12, 19 | Banana Shake Bowls 8, 9, 10, 11, 12, 13, 14, 28 |

| | | | Almonds 8, 9, 10, 11, 12, 14, 18, 22 | | |
|---|---|---|---|---|---|
| Day 42 | Fermented yogurt 6 | Cauliflower Soup 8, 11, 12, 22 | Chicken with Olives, Mustard Greens, and Lemon 11, 18 | Cannellini Bean Soup 20 | Almond Rice Dessert 9, 11, 12, 32 |
| Day 43 | Freekeh Pilaf 3, 9, 10, 11, 13, 14, 18 | Cauliflower Tabbouleh 8, 10, 18 | Chickpeas, Tomato and Kale Stew 13, 25 | Garlicky Broiled Sardines 11, 12, 18 | Dandelion and Strawberry 10, 11, 18 |
| Day 49 | Fresh Tomato Pasta Bowl 8, 11, 12, 18 | Cauliflower and Cherry Tomato Salad 10, 11, 18 | Cold Lemon Squares 8, 9, 10, 11, 12, 13, 14, 28 | Garlic and Lemon Chicken Dish 21 | Banana Shake Bowls 8, 9, 10, 11, 12, 13, 14, 28 |
| Day 50 | Full Eggs in a Squash 8, 11, 12, 18 | Carrot Salad 8, 10, 18 | Gnocchi Ham Olives 8, 11, 18 | Cannellini Beans and Farro Stew 10, 14, 18 | Creamy Mint Strawberry Mix 8, 10, 12, 34 |
| Day 51 | Citrus-Kissed Melon 12, 18 | Citrus Salad 8, 12, 18 | Greek Inspired Rice 10, 12, 18 | Carrot and Bean Stuffed Peppers 8, 9, 14, 18 | Blueberries Stew 8, 10, 12, 33 |
| Day 52 | Garlicky Scrambled Eggs 26 | Cocoa Brownies 9, 10, 11, 13, 30 | Chicken with Greek 8, 11, 18 | Chilled Pea and mint soup 19 | Rhubarb and Apple Cream 9, 11, 12, 32m |
| Day 53 | Fava Beans With Basmati Rice 10, 11, 18 | Coronation Chicken Salad Sirtfood 8, 12, 18 | Chicken with Olives, Mustard Greens, and Lemon 11, 18 | Cinnamon Chickpeas Cookies 9, 10, 11, 13, 30 | Peach Sunrise Smoothie 10, 12, 18 |
| Day 54 | Freekeh Pilaf 3, 9, 10, 11, 13, 14, 18 | Cauliflower Tabbouleh 8, 10, 18 | Chickpeas, Tomato and Kale Stew 13, 25 | Coriander Falafel 8, 9, 10, 11, 12, 13, 18, 25, 18 | Rhubarb and Apple Cream 9, 11, 12, 32 |
| Day 55 | Egg, Pancetta, and Spinach Benedict 8, 10, 17 | Bagna Cauda 9, 10, 11, 13, 18 | Cold Lemon Squares 8, 9, 10, 11, 12, 13, 14, 28 | Cold Lemon Squares 8, 9, 10, 11, 12, 13, 14, 28 | Arugula and Mango 8, 9, 10, 14, 18 |
| Day 56 | Avocado Toast 25 | Baked Black-Eyed Peas 10, 11, 13, 14, 18 | Gnocchi Ham Olives 8, 11, 18 | Cream of Thyme Tomato Soup 19 | Banana Shake Bowls 8, 9, 10, 11, 12, 13, 14, 28 |
| Day 57 | Freekeh Pilaf 3, 9, 10, 11, 13, 14, 18 | Baked Ricotta & Pears 12, 18 | Greek Inspired Rice 10, 12, 18 | Creamy Cauliflower Soup 8, 9, 10, 12, 21, 34 | CaFE Cooler 8, 10, 18 |
| Day 58 | Breakfast Couscous 8, 9, 11, 12, 13, 14, 19, 23, 25 | Banana Cinnamon Cupcakes 9, 11, 13, 31 | Ricotta Stuffed Bell Peppers 12, 18 | Creamy broccoli soup 8, 9, 10, 11, 13, 18 | Cardamom Almond Cream 9, 11, 13, 31 |
| Day 59 | Eggs and Greens 8, 11, 18 | Battuto 7 | Mint avocado chilled soup | Creamy Chicken Soup 11, 13, 26 | Banana Shake Bowls 8, 9, 10, 11, 12, 13, 14, 28 |
| Day 60 | Fava Beans With Basmati Rice 10, 11, 18 | Bulgur Salad with Carrots and Almonds 8, 9, 10, 11, 12, 14, 18, 22 | Pineapple Salsa 8, 11, 12, 18 | Creamy Mint Strawberry Mix 8, 10, 12, 34 | Creamy Mint Strawberry Mix 8, 10, 12, 34 |

| | | | | | |
|---|---|---|---|---|---|
| Day 61 | Fermented yogurt 6 | Cauliflower Soup 8, 11, 12, 22 | Pepper Tapenade 8, 9, 10, 11, 12, 13, 14, 18 | Cucumber Soup 11, 13, 14, 24 | Blueberries Stew 8, 10, 12, 33 |
| Day 62 | Freekeh Pilaf 3, 9, 10, 11, 13, 14, 18 | Cauliflower Tabbouleh 8, 10, 18 | Paprika Chicken Mix 12, 19 | Rice and Veggie Jambalaya 3, 9, 10, 11, 12, 13, 18 | Rhubarb and Apple Cream 9, 11, 12, 32m |
| Day 63 | Fresh Tomato Pasta Bowl 8, 11, 12, 18 | Cauliflower and Cherry Tomato Salad 10, 11, 18 | Olives and Cheese Stuffed Tomatoes 9, 11, 12, 18 | Ricotta Stuffed Bell Peppers 12, 18 | Cardamom Almond Cream 9, 11, 13, 31 |
| Day 64 | Full Eggs in a Squash 8, 11, 12, 18 | Carrot Salad 8, 10, 18 | Braised Cauliflower with White Wine | Mushroom soup 10, 14, 20, 18 | Cinnamon Chickpeas Cookies 9, 10, 11, 13, 30 |
| Day 65 | Citrus-Kissed Melon 12, 18 | Citrus Salad 8, 12, 18 | Rice and Veggie Jambalaya 3, 9, 10, 11, 12, 13, 18 | Mushroom barley soup 8, 9, 12, 18 | Black Tea Cake 9, 10, 11, 14, 29 |
| Day 66 | Garlicky Scrambled Eggs 26 | Cocoa Brownies 9, 10, 11, 13, 30 | Braised Chicken with Mushrooms and Olives 9, 12, 18 | Minty Lentil and Spinach Soup 8, 9, 10, 11, 12, 13, 14, 23 | Banana Shake Bowls 8, 9, 10, 11, 12, 13, 14, 28 |
| Day 67 | Fava Beans With Basmati Rice 10, 11, 18 | Coronation Chicken Salad Sirtfood 8, 12, 18 | Chicken Shawarma 9, 10, 18 | Mint avocado chilled soup 9, 12, 21 | Almond Rice Dessert 9, 11, 12, 32 |
| Day 68 | Freekeh Pilaf 3, 9, 10, 11, 13, 14, 18 | Carrot Salad 8, 10, 18 | Asparagus Avocado Soup 11, 12, 23 | Ratatouille 8, 9, 10, 13, 17, 18 | Dandelion and Strawberry 10, 11, 18 |
| Day 69 | Egg, Pancetta, and Spinach Benedict 8, 10, 17 | Cauliflower Soup 8, 11, 12, 22 | Brown Rice Pilaf with Raisins 11, 13, 18 | Ricotta Stuffed Bell Peppers 12, 18 | Banana Shake Bowls 8, 9, 10, 11, 12, 13, 14, 28 |
| Day 70 | Avocado Toast 25 | Bagna Cauda 9, 10, 11, 13, 18 | Cheesy Stuffed Tomatoes 10, 11, 13, 14, 19 | Guaca Egg Scramble 8, 10, 18 | Creamy Mint Strawberry Mix 8, 10, 12, 34 |
| Day 71 | Egg, Pancetta, and Spinach Benedict 8, 10, 17 | Baked Black-Eyed Peas 10, 11, 13, 14, 18 | Chicken and Leeks Pan 12, 19 | Garlicky Scrambled Eggs 26 | Blueberries Stew 8, 10, 12, 33 |
| Day 72 | Avocado Toast 25 | Baked Ricotta & Pears 12, 18 | Chicken and Peppers Mix 12, 20 | Avocado Toast 25 | Rhubarb and Apple Cream 9, 11, 12, 32m |
| Day 73 | Freekeh Pilaf 3, 9, 10, 11, 13, 14, 18 | Banana Cinnamon Cupcakes 9, 11, 13, 31 | Chicken Shawarma 9, 10, 18 | Belizean Chicken Stew 13, 22 | Peach Sunrise Smoothie 10, 12, 18 |
| Day 74 | Breakfast Couscous 8, 9, 11, 12, 13, 14, 19, 23, 25 | Battuto 7 | Chicken Skillet 9, 11, 12, 13, 18 | Garlic and Lemon Chicken Dish 21 | Rhubarb and Apple Cream 9, 11, 12, 32 |
| Day 75 | Eggs and Greens 8, 11, 18 | Bulgur Salad with Carrots and Almonds 8, 9, 10, 11, 12, 14, 18, 22 | Chicken Stuffed Peppers 8, 12, 18 | Chicken and Peppers Mix 12, 20 | Arugula and Mango 8, 9, 10, 14, 18 |

| Day | | | | | |
|---|---|---|---|---|---|
| Day 76 | Fava Beans With Basmati Rice 10, 11, 18 | Cauliflower Soup 8, 11, 12, 22 | Chicken with Greek 8, 11, 18 | Chicken and Leeks Pan 12, 19 | Banana Shake Bowls 8, 9, 10, 11, 12, 13, 14, 28 |
| Day 77 | Fermented yogurt 6 | Cauliflower Tabbouleh 8, 10, 18 | Chicken with Olives, Mustard Greens, and Lemon 11, 18 | Cannellini Bean Soup 20 | CaFE Cooler 8, 10, 18 |
| Day 78 | Freekeh Pilaf 3, 9, 10, 11, 13, 14, 18 | Cauliflower and Cherry Tomato Salad 10, 11, 18 | Chickpeas, Tomato and Kale Stew 13, 25 | Garlicky Broiled Sardines 11, 12, 18 | Cardamom Almond Cream 9, 11, 13, 31 |
| Day 79 | Fresh Tomato Pasta Bowl 8, 11, 12, 18 | Carrot Salad 8, 10, 18 | Cold Lemon Squares 8, 9, 10, 11, 12, 13, 14, 28 | Garlic and Lemon Chicken Dish 21 | Banana Shake Bowls 8, 9, 10, 11, 12, 13, 14, 28 |
| Day 80 | Full Eggs in a Squash 8, 11, 12, 18 | Citrus Salad 8, 12, 18 | Gnocchi Ham Olives 8, 11, 18 | Cannellini Beans and Farro Stew 10, 14, 18 | Creamy Mint Strawberry Mix 8, 10, 12, 34 |
| Day 81 | Citrus-Kissed Melon 12, 18 | Cocoa Brownies 9, 10, 11, 13, 30 | Greek Inspired Rice 10, 12, 18 | Carrot and Bean Stuffed Peppers 8, 9, 14, 18 | Blueberries Stew 8, 10, 12, 33 |
| Day 82 | Garlicky Scrambled Eggs 26 | Coronation Chicken Salad Sirtfood 8, 12, 18 | Chicken with Greek 8, 11, 18 | Chilled Pea and mint soup 19 | Rhubarb and Apple Cream 9, 11, 12, 32m |
| Day 83 | Fava Beans With Basmati Rice 10, 11, 18 | Arugula and Mango Salad | Chicken with Olives, Mustard Greens, and Lemon 11, 18 | Cinnamon Chickpeas Cookies 9, 10, 11, 13, 30 | Cardamom Almond Cream 9, 11, 13, 31 |
| Day 84 | Freekeh Pilaf 3, 9, 10, 11, 13, 14, 18 | Bagna Cauda 9, 10, 11, 13, 18 | Chickpeas, Tomato and Kale Stew 13, 25 | Coriander Falafel 8, 9, 10, 11, 12, 13, 18, 25, 18 | Cinnamon Chickpeas Cookies 9, 10, 11, 13, 30 |
| Day 85 | Egg, Pancetta, and Spinach Benedict 8, 10, 17 | Baked Black-Eyed Peas 10, 11, 13, 14, 18 | Cold Lemon Squares 8, 9, 10, 11, 12, 13, 14, 28 | Cold Lemon Squares 8, 9, 10, 11, 12, 13, 14, 28 | Black Tea Cake 9, 10, 11, 14, 29 |
| Day 86 | Avocado Toast 25 | Baked Ricotta & Pears 12, 18 | Gnocchi Ham Olives 8, 11, 18 | Cream of Thyme Tomato Soup 19 | Banana Shake Bowls 8, 9, 10, 11, 12, 13, 14, 28 |
| Day 87 | Freekeh Pilaf 3, 9, 10, 11, 13, 14, 18 | Banana Cinnamon Cupcakes 9, 11, 13, 31 | Greek Inspired Rice 10, 12, 18 | Creamy Cauliflower Soup 8, 9, 10, 12, 21, 34 | Almond Rice Dessert 9, 11, 12, 32 |
| Day 88 | Breakfast Couscous 8, 9, 11, 12, 13, 14, 19, 23, 25 | Battuto 7 | Ricotta Stuffed Bell Peppers 12, 18 | Creamy broccoli soup 8, 9, 10, 11, 13, 18 | Dandelion and Strawberry 10, 11, 18 |
| Day 89 | Eggs and Greens 8, 11, 18 | Bulgur Salad with Carrots and Almonds 8, 9, 10, 11, 12, 14, 18, 22 | Cold Lemon Squares 8, 9, 10, 11, 12, 13, 14, 28 | Creamy Chicken Soup 11, 13, 26 | Banana Shake Bowls 8, 9, 10, 11, 12, 13, 14, 28 |
| Day 90 | Fava Beans With Basmati Rice 10, 11, 18 | Cauliflower Soup 8, 11, 12, 22 | Pineapple Salsa 8, 11, 12, 18 | Creamy Mint Strawberry Mix 8, 10, 12, 34 | Creamy Mint Strawberry Mix 8, 10, 12, 34 |

| Day | Breakfast | Snack | Lunch | Snack | Dinner |
|---|---|---|---|---|---|
| Day 91 | Fermented yogurt 6 | Cauliflower Tabbouleh 8, 10, 18 | Pepper Tapenade 8, 9, 10, 11, 12, 13, 14, 18 | Cucumber Soup 11, 13, 14, 24 | Blueberries Stew 8, 10, 12, 33 |
| Day 92 | Freekeh Pilaf 3, 9, 10, 11, 13, 14, 18 | Cauliflower and Cherry Tomato Salad 10, 11, 18 | Paprika Chicken Mix 12, 19 | Rice and Veggie Jambalaya 3, 9, 10, 11, 12, 13, 18 | Rhubarb and Apple Cream 9, 11, 12, 32m |
| Day 93 | Fresh Tomato Pasta Bowl 8, 11, 12, 18 | Carrot Salad 8, 10, 18 | Olives and Cheese Stuffed Tomatoes 9, 11, 12, 18 | Ricotta Stuffed Bell Peppers 12, 18 | Peach Sunrise Smoothie 10, 12, 18 |
| Day 94 | Full Eggs in a Squash 8, 11, 12, 18 | Citrus Salad 8, 12, 18 | Braised Cauliflower with White Wine | Mushroom soup 10, 14, 20, 18 O | Rhubarb and Apple Cream 9, 11, 12, 32 |
| Day 95 | Egg, Pancetta, and Spinach Benedict 8, 10, 17 | Banana Cinnamon Cupcakes 9, 11, 13, 31 | Rice and Veggie Jambalaya 3, 9, 10, 11, 12, 13, 18 | Mushroom barley soup 8, 9, 12, 18 | Arugula and Mango 8, 9, 10, 14, 18 |
| Day 96 | Avocado Toast 25 | Bagna Cauda 9, 10, 11, 13, 18 | Braised Chicken with Mushrooms and Olives 9, 12, 18 | Minty Lentil and Spinach Soup 8, 9, 10, 11, 12, 13, 14, 23 | Banana Shake Bowls 8, 9, 10, 11, 12, 13, 14, 28 |
| Day 97 | Freekeh Pilaf 3, 9, 10, 11, 13, 14, 18 | Baked Black-Eyed Peas 10, 11, 13, 14, 18 | Chicken Shawarma 9, 10, 18 | Mint avocado chilled soup 9, 12, 21 | CaFE Cooler 8, 10, 18 |
| Day 98 | Breakfast Couscous 8, 9, 11, 12, 13, 14, 19, 23, 25 | Baked Ricotta & Pears 12, 18 | Asparagus Avocado Soup 11, 12, 23 | Ratatouille 8, 9, 10, 13, 17, 18 | Cardamom Almond Cream 9, 11, 13, 31 |
| Day 99 | Eggs and Greens 8, 11, 18 | Banana Cinnamon Cupcakes 9, 11, 13, 31 | Brown Rice Pilaf with Raisins 11, 13, 18 | Ricotta Stuffed Bell Peppers 12, 18 | Banana Shake Bowls 8, 9, 10, 11, 12, 13, 14, 28 |
| Day 100 | Fava Beans With Basmati Rice 10, 11, 18 | Battuto 7 | Cheesy Stuffed Tomatoes 10, 11, 13, 14, 19 | Guaca Egg Scramble 8, 10, 18 | Creamy Mint Strawberry Mix 8, 10, 12, 34 |
| Day 101 | Fermented yogurt 6 | Bulgur Salad with Carrots and Almonds 8, 9, 10, 11, 12, 14, 18, 22 | Chicken and Leeks Pan 12, 19 | Garlicky Scrambled Eggs 26 | Blueberries Stew 8, 10, 12, 33 |
| Day 102 | Freekeh Pilaf 3, 9, 10, 11, 13, 14, 18 | Cauliflower Soup 8, 11, 12, 22 | Chicken and Peppers Mix 12, 20 | Avocado Toast 25 | Rhubarb and Apple Cream 9, 11, 12, 32m |
| Day 103 | Fresh Tomato Pasta Bowl 8, 11, 12, 18 | Cauliflower Tabbouleh 8, 10, 18 | Chicken Shawarma 9, 10, 18 | Egg, Pancetta, and Spinach Benedict 8, 10, 17 | Cardamom Almond Cream 9, 11, 13, 31 |
| Day 104 | Full Eggs in a Squash 8, 11, 12, 18 | Cauliflower and Cherry Tomato Salad 10, 11, 18 | Chicken Skillet 9, 11, 12, 13, 18 | Easy Tzatziki Sauce 8, 9, 10, 11, 12, 13, 18, 26, 34 | Cinnamon Chickpeas Cookies 9, 10, 11, 13, 30 |
| Day 105 | Citrus-Kissed Melon 12, 18 | Carrot Salad 8, 10, 18 | Chicken Stuffed Peppers 8, 12, 18 | Easy Cauliflower Soup 3, 9, 13, 14 | Black Tea Cake 9, 10, 11, 14, 29 |

# Mediterranean Diet Recipes

# Breakfast Brunch AND Smoothies

## Egg, Pancetta, and Spinach Benedict

**PREPARATION TIME: 16 MINUTES**
**COOKING TIME: 24 MINUTES**
**SERVINGS: 2**

### INGREDIENTS:
- 1/4 cup diced pancetta
- 2 cups baby spinach leaves
- 1/4 teaspoon freshly ground black pepper
- 1/4 teaspoon salt, or to taste
- 2 large eggs
- Extra-virgin olive oil (optional)
- 1 whole-grain English muffin, toasted

### DIRECTIONS:
- In a medium, heavy skillet, brown the pancetta over medium-low heat for about 5 minutes, stirring frequently, until crisp on all sides.
- Stir in the spinach, pepper, and salt if desired (it may not need any, depending on how salty the pancetta is). Cook, stirring occasionally, for 5 minutes. Transfer the mixture to a medium bowl.
- Crack the eggs into the same pan (add olive oil if the pan looks dry), and cook until the whites are just opaque, 3 to 4 minutes. Carefully flip the eggs and continue cooking for 30 seconds to 1 minute until done to your preferred degree for over-easy eggs.
- Situate muffin half on each of 2 plates and top each with half of the spinach mixture and 1 egg, yolk side up. Pierce the yolks just before serving.

Nutrition: 391 calories 21g fats 15g protein

## Banana Nut Oatmeal

**PREPARATION TIME: 5 MINUTES**
**COOKING TIME: 3 MINUTES**
**SERVINGS: 1**

### INGREDIENTS:
- Peeled Banana
- 1/2 cup of Skim Milk
- 1/4 cup of Quick Cooking Oats
- 3 tbsp. of Honey
- 2 tbsp. of Chopped Walnuts 1 tsp. of Flax Seeds

### DIRECTIONS:
- In a microwave-safe dish, combine the milk, rice, sugar, walnuts, banana, and flax seeds. Cook for 3 minutes in the oven, then mash the banana with a fork and whisk it into the mixture.
- Serve and Enjoy!

Nutrition: 391 calories 21g fats 15g protein

## Heart-Healthful Trail Mix

PREPARATION TIME: 8 MINUTES
COOKING TIME: 32 MINUTES
SERVINGS: 2

- 1 cup raw almonds
- 1 cup walnut halves
- 1 cup pumpkin seeds
- 1 cup dried apricots, cut into thin strips
- 1 cup dried cherries, roughly chopped
- 1 cup golden raisins
- 2 tablespoons extra-virgin olive oil
- 1 teaspoon salt

DIRECTIONS:
- Preheat the oven to 300°F. Line a baking sheet with aluminum foil.
- In a large bowl, mix almonds, walnuts, pumpkin seeds, apricots, cherries, and raisins. Pour the olive oil over all and toss well with clean hands. Add salt and toss again to distribute.
- Fill in the nut mixture onto the baking sheet in a single layer and bake until the fruits begin to brown, about 30 minutes. Chill on the baking sheet to room temperature.
- Store in a large airtight container or zipper-top plastic bag.

Nutrition: 109 calories 7g fats 1g protein

## CaFE Cooler

PREPARATION TIME: 16 MINUTES
COOKING TIME: 0 MINUTE
SERVINGS: 2

- Ice cubes
- 2 cups of low-fat milk
- 1/2 teaspoon ground cinnamon
- 1/2 teaspoon pure vanilla extract
- 1 cup espresso, cooled to room temperature
- 4 teaspoons sugar (optional)

DIRECTIONS:
- Fill four tall glasses with ice cubes.
- In a blender, combine the milk, cinnamon, and vanilla and blend until frothy.
- Pour the milk over the ice cubes and top each drink with one-quarter of the espresso. If using sugar, stir it into the espresso until it has dissolved. Serve immediately, with chilled teaspoons for stirring.

Nutrition: 93 calories 7g fats 1g protein

## Savory Avocado Spread

PREPARATION TIME: 17 MINUTES
COOKING TIME: 0 MINUTE
SERVINGS: 2

### INGREDIENTS:
- 1 ripe avocado
- 1 teaspoon lemon juice
- 6 boneless sardine filets
- 1/4 cup diced sweet white onion
- 1 stalk celery, diced
- 1/2 teaspoon salt
- 1/4 teaspoon black pepper

### DIRECTIONS:
- In a blender, pulse avocado, lemon juice, and sardine filets
- Ladle the mixture into a small bowl and stir in the onion, celery, salt, and pepper. Mix well with a fork and serve as desired.

Nutrition: 109 calories 15g fats 6g protein

## Cheesy Stuffed Tomatoes

PREPARATION TIME: 6 MINUTES
COOKING TIME: 22 MINUTES
SERVINGS: 2

### INGREDIENTS:
- 4 large, ripe tomatoes
- 1 tablespoon extra-virgin olive oil
- 2 garlic cloves, minced
- 1/2 cup diced yellow onion
- 1/2-pound cremini mushrooms
- 1 tablespoon chopped fresh basil
- 1 tablespoon chopped fresh oregano
- 1/2 teaspoon salt
- 1/4 teaspoon freshly ground black pepper
- 1 cup shredded part-skim mozzarella cheese
- 1 tablespoon grated Parmesan cheese

### DIRECTIONS:
- Preheat the oven to 375°F. Line a baking sheet with aluminum foil.
- Cut a sliver from the bottom of each tomato so they will stand upright without wobbling. Cut a 1/2-inch slice from the top of each tomato and use a spoon to gently remove most of the pulp, placing it in a medium bowl. Place the tomatoes on the baking sheet.
- In a skillet, cook olive oil over medium heat. Sauté the garlic, onion, mushrooms, basil, and oregano for 5 minutes, and season with salt and pepper.
- Transfer the mixture to the bowl and blend well with the tomato pulp. Stir in the mozzarella cheese.
- Fill each tomato loosely with the mixture, top with Parmesan cheese, and bake until the cheese is bubbly, 15 to 20 minutes. Serve immediately.

Nutrition: 201 calories 19g fats 6g protein

## Gnocchi Ham Olives

**PREPARATION TIME: 5 MINUTES**
**COOKING TIME: 15 MINUTES**
**SERVINGS:**

### INGREDIENTS:
- 2 tablespoons of olive oil
- 1 medium-sized onion chopped up
- 3 minced cloves of garlic
- 1 medium-sized red pepper completely deseeded and finely chopped
- 1 cup of tomato puree
- 2 tablespoons of tomato paste
- 1 pound of gnocchi
- 1 cup of coarsely chopped turkey ham
- ½ cup of sliced pitted olives
- 1 teaspoon of Italian seasoning
- Salt as needed
- Freshly ground black pepper
- Bunch of fresh basil leaves

### DIRECTIONS:
- Take a medium-sized sauce pan and place over medium-high heat. Pour some olive oil and heat it up. Toss in the bell pepper, onion, and garlic and sauté for 2 minutes.
- Pour in the tomato puree, gnocchi, and tomato paste, and add the turkey ham, Italian seasoning, and olives. Simmer the whole mix for 15 minutes, making sure to stir from time to time.
- Season the mix with some pepper and salt. Once done, transfer the mix to a dish and garnish with some basil leaves. Serve hot and have fun.

Nutrition: Calories: 335 Fat: 12g Carbohydrates: 45g Protein: 15g

## Eggs and Greens

**READY IN ABOUT 20 MINUTES**
**SERVING 2**

### INGREDIENTS
- 1 tablespoon of olive oil
- 2 cups of chopped and steamed rainbow chard
- 1 cup of fresh spinach
- 1/2 cup of arugula
- 2 cloves of garlic, minced
- 4 pounded eggs
- 1/2 cup sliced Cheddar cheese
- To taste: salt or black pepper

### INSTRUCTIONS
- Heat oil over medium-high heat in a skillet. Sauté the spinach, chard, and arugula for around 3 minutes until tender. Add garlic; cook and mix for around 2 minutes, until fragrant.
- In a cup, mix the eggs and cheese; pour in the chard mix. Cover and cook for 5 to 7
- minutes until set. Season with pepper and salt.

Per serving: Kcal 333, Fat: 26. 2g, Net Carbs: 4. 2g, Protein: 21g

## Spicy Early Morning Seafood Risotto

**PREPARATION TIME: 5 MINUTES**
**COOKING TIME: 15 MINUTES**
**SERVINGS:**

### INGREDIENTS:
- 3 cups of clam juice
- 2 cups of water
- 2 tablespoons of olive oil
- 1 medium-sized chopped up onion
- 2 minced cloves of garlic
- 1 ½ cups of Arborio Rice
- ½ cup of dry white wine
- 1 teaspoon of Saffron
- ½ teaspoon of ground cumin
- ½ teaspoon of paprika
- 1 pound of marinara seafood mix
- Salt as needed
- Ground pepper as needed

### DIRECTIONS:
- Place a saucepan over high heat and pour in your clam juice with water and bring the mixture to a boil. Remove the heat.
- Take a heavy-bottomed saucepan and stir fry your garlic and onion in oil over medium heat until a nice fragrance comes off.
- Add in the rice and keep stirring for 2-3 minutes until the rice has been fully covered with the oil. Pour the wine, and then add the saffron.
- Keep stirring constantly until it is fully absorbed. Add in the cumin, clam juice, and paprika mixture 1 cup at a time, making sure to keep stirring it from time to time.
- Cook the rice for 20 minutes until perfect. Finally, add the seafood marinara mix and cook for another 5-7 minutes.
- Season with some pepper and salt. Transfer the meal to a serving dish. Serve hot.

Nutrition: Calories: 386 Fat: 7g Carbohydrates: 55g Protein: 21g

## Sweet Potato Tart

**PREPARATION TIME: 10 MINUTES**
**COOKING TIME: 1 HOUR AND 10 MINUTES SERVINGS:**

### INGREDIENTS:
- 2 pounds of sweet potatoes, peeled and cubed
- ¼ cup olive oil + a drizzle
- 7 oz. feta cheese, crumbled
- 1 yellow onion, chopped
- 2 eggs, whisked
- ¼ cup almond milk
- 1 tbsp. herbs de Provence
- A pinch of salt and black pepper
- 6 phyllo sheets
- 1 tbsp. parmesan, grated

### DIRECTIONS:
- In a bowl, combine the potatoes with half of the oil, salt, and pepper, toss, spread on a baking sheet lined with parchment paper, and roast at 400F for 25 minutes.
- Meanwhile, heat a pan with half of the remaining oil over medium heat, add the onion, and sauté for 5 minutes.
- In a bowl, combine the eggs with the milk, feta, herbs, salt, pepper, onion, sweet potatoes, and the rest of the oil and toss.
- Arrange the phyllo sheets in a tart pan and brush them with a drizzle of oil. Add the sweet potato mix and spread it well into the pan.
- Sprinkle the parmesan on top and bake covered with tin foil at 350F for 20 minutes. Remove the tin foil, bake the tart for 20 minutes more, cool it down, slice, and serve for breakfast.

Nutrition: Calories 476 Fat: 16.8g Carbs: 68.8g Protein: 13.9g

## Rocket Tomatoes and Mushroom Frittata

**PREPARATION TIME:** 5 MINUTES
**COOKING TIME:** 15 MINUTES
**SERVINGS:**

### INGREDIENTS:
- 2 tablespoons of butter (replace with canola oil for full effect)
- 1 chopped up medium-sized onion
- 2 minced cloves of garlic
- 1 cup of coarsely chopped baby rocket tomato
- 1 cup of sliced button mushrooms
- 6 large pieces of eggs
- ½ cup of skim milk
- 1 teaspoon of dried rosemary
- Salt as needed
- Ground black pepper as needed

### DIRECTIONS:
- Pre-heat your oven to 400 degrees Fahrenheit. Take a large oven-proof pan and place it over medium heat. Heat up some oil.
- Stir fry your garlic and onion for about 2 minutes. Add the mushroom, rosemary, and rockets and cook for 3 minutes. Take a medium-sized bowl and beat your eggs alongside the milk.
- Season it with some salt and pepper. Pour the egg mixture into your pan with the vegetables and sprinkle some Parmesan.
- Reduce the heat to low and cover with the lid. Let it cook for 3 minutes. Transfer the pan to your oven and bake for 10 minutes until fully settled.
- Reduce the heat to low and cover with your lid. Let it cook for 3 minutes. Transfer the pan to your oven and then bake for another 10 minutes. Serve hot.

Nutrition: Calories: 189 Fat: 13g Carbohydrates: 6g Protein: 12g

## Full Eggs in a Squash

**PREPARATION TIME:** 15 MINUTES
**COOKING TIME:** 20 MINUTES
**SERVINGS:**

### INGREDIENTS:
- 2 acorn squash
- 6 whole eggs
- 2 tablespoons extra virgin olive oil
- Salt and pepper as needed
- 5-6 pitted dates
- 8 walnut halves
- A fresh bunch of parsley

### DIRECTIONS:
- Pre-heat your oven to 375 degrees Fahrenheit. Slice squash crosswise and prepare 3 slices with holes. While slicing the squash, make sure that each slice has a measurement of ¾ inch thickness.
- Remove the seeds from the slices. Take a baking sheet and line it with parchment paper. Transfer the slices to your baking sheet and season them with salt and pepper.
- Bake in your oven for 20 minutes. Chop the walnuts and dates on your cutting board. Take the baking dish out of the oven and drizzle slices with olive oil.
- Crack an egg into each of the holes in the slices and season with pepper and salt. Sprinkle the chopped walnuts on top. Bake for 10 minutes more. Garnish with parsley and add maple syrup.

Nutrition: Calories: 198 Fat: 12g Carbohydrates: 17g Protein: 8g

## Fresh Tomato Pasta Bowl

**PREPARATION TIME: 7 MINUTES**
**COOKING TIME: 26 MINUTES**
**SERVINGS: 2**

### INGREDIENTS:
- 8 ounces whole-grain linguine
- 1 tablespoon extra-virgin olive oil
- 2 garlic cloves, minced
- 1/4 cup chopped yellow onion
- 1 teaspoon chopped fresh oregano
- 1/2 teaspoon salt
- 1/4 teaspoon freshly ground black pepper
- 1 teaspoon tomato paste
- 8 ounces cherry tomatoes, halved
- 1/2 cup grated Parmesan cheese
- 1 tablespoon chopped fresh parsley

### DIRECTIONS:
- Boil water at high heat and cook the linguine according to the package instructions until al dente. Set aside a half cup of pasta water. Do not rinse the pasta.
- In a large, heavy skillet, heat the olive oil over medium-high heat. Sauté the garlic, onion, and oregano for 5 minutes.
- Add the salt, pepper, tomato paste, and 1/4 cup of the reserved pasta water. Stir well and cook for 1 minute.
- Stir in the tomatoes and cooked pasta, tossing everything well to coat. Add more pasta water if needed.
- To serve, top with Parmesan cheese and parsley.

Nutrition: 391 calories 28g fats 9g protein

## Date and Walnut Overnight Oats

**PREPARATION TIME: 5 MINUTES**
**COOKING TIME: 20 MINUTES**
**SERVINGS: 2**

### INGREDIENTS:
- ¼ Cup Greek Yogurt, Plain
- 1/3 cup of yogurt
- 2/3 cup of oats
- 1 cup of milk
- 2 tsp date syrup, or you can also use maple syrup or honey
- 1 mashed banana
- ¼ tsp cinnamon
- ¼ cup walnuts
- pinch of salt (approx. 1/8 tsp)

### DIRECTIONS:
- Firstly, get a mason jar or a small bowl and add all the ingredients. After that, stir and mix all the ingredients well. Cover it securely, and cool it in a refrigerator overnight.
- After that, take it out the next morning, add more liquid or cinnamon if required, and serve cold. (However, you can also microwave it for people with a warmer palate.

Nutrition: Calories: 350 Protein: 14 g Fat: 12 g Carbs: 49 g

## Peach Sunrise Smoothie

**PREPARATION TIME: 6 MINUTES**
**COOKING TIME: 0 MINUTE**
**SERVINGS: 2**

### DIRECTIONS:
- Incorporate all **ingredients** in a blender and blend until thick and creamy. Serve immediately.

### INGREDIENTS:
- 1 large unpeeled peach, pitted and sliced (about 1/2 cup)
- 6 ounces vanilla or peach low-fat Greek yogurt
- 2 tablespoons low-fat milk
- 6 to 8 ice cubes

Nutrition: 98 calories 16g fats 3g protein

## Tomato and Dill Frittata

**PREPARATION TIME: 5 MINUTES**
**COOKING TIME: 10 MINUTES**
**SERVINGS: 4**

### DIRECTIONS:
- Pre-heat your oven to a temperature of 400 degrees Fahrenheit. Take a large-sized ovenproof pan and heat up your olive oil over medium-high heat. Toss in the onion, garlic, and tomatoes and stir fry them for 4 minutes.
- While they are being cooked, take a bowl and beat together your eggs, half and half cream, and season the mix with some pepper and salt.
- Pour the mixture into the pan with your vegetables and top it with crumbled feta cheese and dill weed. Cover it with the lid and let it cook for 3 minutes.
- Place the pan inside your oven and let it bake for 10 minutes. Serve hot.

### INGREDIENTS:
- 2 tablespoons olive oil
- 1 medium onion, chopped
- 1 teaspoon garlic, minced
- 2 medium tomatoes, chopped
- 6 large eggs
- ½ cup half and half
- ½ cup feta cheese, crumbled
- ¼ cup dill weed
- Salt as needed
- Ground black pepper as needed

Nutrition: Calories: 191 Fat: 15g Carbohydrates: 6g Protein: 9g

## Baked Ricotta & Pears

**PREPARATION TIME: 15 MINUTES**
**COOKING TIME: 30 MINUTES**
**SERVINGS: 4**

### INGREDIENTS:
- ¼ cup White whole wheat flour
- 1 tbsp. Sugar
- ¼ tsp Nutmeg
- Ricotta cheese
- 16 oz. container whole-milk
- 2 Large eggs
- 1 Diced pear
- 2 tbsp. Water
- 1 tsp. Vanilla extract
- 1 tbsp. Honey
- Also Needed: 4 - 6 oz. ramekins

### DIRECTIONS:
- Warm the oven to 400°F. Lightly spritz the ramekins with a cooking oil spray. Whisk the flour, nutmeg, sugar, vanilla, eggs, and ricotta together in a large mixing container.
- Spoon the fixings into the dishes. Bake them for 20 to 25 minutes or until they're firm and set. Transfer them to the countertop and wait for them to cool.
- In a saucepan, using the medium temperature setting, toss the cored and diced pear into the water for about ten minutes until it's slightly softened.
- Take the pan from the burner and stir in the honey. Serve the ricotta ramekins with the warm pear when it's ready.

Nutrition: Calories 312 Protein: 17g Carbs: 0g Fat: 17g

## Coconut Porridge

**PREPARATION TIME: 15 MINUTES**
**COOKING TIME: 0 MINUTES**
**SERVINGS: 6**

### INGREDIENTS:
- Powdered erythritol as needed
- 1 ½ cups almond milk, unsweetened
- 2 tablespoons vanilla protein powder
- 3 tablespoons Golden Flaxseed meal
- 2 tablespoons coconut flour

### DIRECTIONS:
- Take a bowl and mix in flaxseed meal, protein powder, and coconut flour and mix well. Add mix to a saucepan (placed over medium heat).
- Add almond milk and stir; let the mixture thicken. Add your desired amount of sweetener and serve. Enjoy!

Nutrition: Calories: 259 Fat: 13g Carbohydrates: 5g Protein: 16g

## Citrus-Kissed Melon

PREPARATION TIME: 11 MINUTES
COOKING TIME: 0 MINUTE
SERVINGS: 2

DIRECTIONS:
- In a large bowl, incorporate melon cubes. In a bowl, blend the orange juice, lime juice, and orange zest and pour over the fruit.
- Cover and let cool, stirring occasionally.
- Serve chilled.

INGREDIENTS:
- 2 cups cubed melon
- 2 cups cubed cantaloupe
- 1/2 cup freshly squeezed orange juice
- 1/4 cup freshly squeezed lime juice
- 1 tablespoon orange zest

Nutrition: 101 calories 11g fats 2g protein

## Garlicky Broiled Sardines

PREPARATION TIME: 6 MINUTES
COOKING TIME: 31 MINUTES
SERVINGS: 2

DIRECTIONS:
- Preheat the broiler. Line a baking dish with aluminum foil. Lay sardines in a single layer on the foil.
- Combine the olive oil (if using), garlic, and red pepper flakes in a small bowl and spoon over each sardine. Season with salt and pepper.
- Broil just until sizzling, 2 to 3 minutes.
- To serve, place 4 sardines on each plate and top with any remaining garlic mixture that has collected in the baking dish.

INGREDIENTS:
- 4 (3.25-ounce) cans of sardines packed in water or olive oil
- 2 tablespoons extra-virgin olive oil
- 4 garlic cloves, minced
- 1/2 teaspoon red pepper flakes
- 1/2 teaspoon salt
- 1/4 teaspoon black pepper

Nutrition: 308 calories 17g fats 9g protein

## Mediterranean Eggs

**PREPARATION TIME: 15 MINUTES**
**COOKING TIME: 20 MINUTES**
**SERVINGS: 2**

### INGREDIENTS:
- 5 tbsp. of divided olive oil
- 2 diced medium-sized Spanish onions
- 2 diced red bell peppers
- 2 minced cloves of garlic
- 1 teaspoon cumin seeds
- 4 diced large ripe tomatoes
- 1 tablespoon of honey
- Salt
- Freshly ground black pepper
- 1/3 cup crumbled feta
- 4 eggs
- 1 teaspoon zaatar spice
- Grilled pita during serving

### DIRECTIONS:
- Add 3 tablespoons of olive oil into a pan and heat it over medium heat. Along with the oil, sauté the cumin seeds, onions, garlic, and red pepper for a few minutes.
- After that, add the diced tomatoes and salt and pepper to taste and cook them for about 10 minutes till they come together and form a light sauce.
- With that, half the preparation is already done. Now you just have to break the eggs directly into the sauce and poach them.
- However, you must keep in mind to cook the egg whites but keep the yolks still runny. This takes about 8 to 10 minutes.
- While plating, adds some feta and olive oil with zaatar spice to further enhance the flavors. Once done, serve with grilled pita.

Nutrition: Calories: 304 Protein: 12 g Fat: 16 g Carbs: 28 g

## Mediterranean Feta and Quinoa E

**PREPARATION TIME: 15 MINUTES**
**COOKING TIME: 15 MINUTES**
**SERVINGS: 12**

### INGREDIENTS:
- 2 cups baby spinach finely chopped
- 1 cup chopped or sliced cherry tomatoes
- 1/2 cup finely chopped onion
- 1 tablespoon chopped fresh oregano
- 1 cup crumbled feta cheese
- 1/2 cup chopped {pitted} kalamata olives
- 2 teaspoons high oleic sunflower oil
- 1 cup cooked quinoa
- 8 eggs
- 1/4 teaspoon salt

### DIRECTIONS:
- Preheat the oven to 350 degrees Fahrenheit, and then prepare 12 silicone muffin holders on the baking sheet, or just grease a 12-cup muffin tin with oil and set aside.
- Finely chop the vegetables, and then heat the skillet to medium. After that, add the vegetable oil and onions and sauté for 2 minutes.
- Then, add tomatoes and sauté for another minute, then add spinach and sauté until wilted, about 1 minute.
- Place the beaten egg into a bowl and then add lots of vegetables like feta cheese, quinoa, veggie mixture as well as salt, and then stir well until everything is properly combined.
- Pour the ready mixture into greased muffin tins or silicone cups, dividing the mixture equally. Then, bake it in an oven for 30 minutes or so.

Nutrition: Calories: 113 Protein: 6 g Fat: 7 g Carbs: 5 g

# Appetizers, Dips AND Snacks

## Guaca Egg Scramble

PREPARATION TIME: 8 MINUTES
COOKING TIME: 15 MINUTES
SERVINGS: 2

### INGREDIENTS

- 4 eggs, beaten
- 1 white onion, diced
- 1 tablespoon avocado oil
- 1 avocado, finely chopped
- ½ teaspoon chili flakes
- 1 oz. Cheddar cheese, shredded
- ½ teaspoon salt
- 1 tablespoon fresh parsley

### DIRECTIONS:

- Pour avocado oil into the skillet and bring it to a boil. Then add diced onion and roast it until it is light brown. Meanwhile, mix up together chili flakes, beaten eggs, and salt.
- Fill the egg mixture over the cooked onion and cook the mixture for 1 minute over medium heat. After this, scramble the eggs well with the help of the fork or spatula. Cook the eggs until they are solid but soft.
- After this, add chopped avocado and shredded cheese. Stir the scramble well and transfer it to the serving plates. Sprinkle the meal with fresh parsley.

Nutrition: 236 Calories 20g Fat 4g Carbohydrates 8.6g Protein

## Easy Tzatziki Sauce

PREP TIME: 5 MINUTES
COOK TIME: 0 MINUTES
SERVES 2

### INGREDIENTS:

- 1 medium cucumber, peeled, seeded, and diced
- ½ teaspoon salt, divided, plus more
- ½ cup plain, unsweetened, full-fat Greek yogurt
- ½ lemon, juiced
- 1 tablespoon chopped fresh parsley
- ½ teaspoon dried minced garlic
- ½ teaspoon dried dill
- Freshly ground black pepper, to taste

### DIRECTIONS:

- Put the cucumber in a colander. Sprinkle with ¼ teaspoon of salt and toss. Let the cucumber rest at room temperature in the colander for 30 minutes.
- Rinse the cucumber in cool water and place it in a single layer on several layers of paper towels to remove the excess liquid.
- In a food processor, pulse the cucumber to chop finely and drain off any extra fluid.
- Pour bthe cucumber into a mixing bowl and add the yogurt, lemon juice, parsley, garlic, dill, and the remaining ¼ teaspoon of salt. Season with salt and pepper to taste, and whisk the ingredients together. Refrigerate in an airtight container.

Nutrition: calories: 77 fat: 3g protein: 6g carbs: 6g fiber: 1g sodium: 607mg

## Cucumber Yogurt Dip

PREP TIME: 5 MINUTES
COOK TIME: 0 MINUTES
SERVES 2 TO 3

DIRECTIONS:
- In a food processor, combine the yogurt, cucumber, lemon juice, mint, and garlic. Pulse several times to combine, leaving noticeable cucumber chunks.
- Taste and season with salt and pepper.

INGREDIENTS:
- 1 cup plain, unsweetened, full-fat Greek yogurt
- ½ cup cucumber, peeled, seeded, and diced
- 1 tablespoon freshly squeezed lemon juice
- 1 tablespoon chopped fresh mint
- 1 small garlic clove, minced
- Salt and freshly ground black pepper to taste

Nutrition: calories: 128 fat: 6g protein: 11g carbs: 7g fiber: 0g sodium: 47mg

## Arugula Walnut Pesto

PREP TIME: 5 MINUTES
COOK TIME: 0 MINUTES
SERVES 8 TO 10

DIRECTIONS:
- In a food processor, combine the arugula, walnuts, cheese, and garlic and process until very finely chopped. Add the salt. With the processor running, stream in the olive oil until well blended.
- If the mixture seems too thick, add warm water, 1 tablespoon at a time, until smooth and creamy. Store in a sealed container in the refrigerator.

INGREDIENTS:
- 6 cups packed arugula
- 1 cup chopped walnuts
- ½ cup shredded Parmesan cheese
- 2 garlic cloves, peeled
- ½ teaspoon salt
- 1 cup extra-virgin olive oil

Per Serving (2 tablespoons): calories: 296 fat: 31g protein: 4g carbs: 2g fiber: 1g sodium: 206mg

## Tarragon Grapefruit Dressing

**PREP TIME: 5 MINUTES**
**COOK TIME: 0 MINUTES**
**SERVES 4 TO 6**

### INGREDIENTS:
- ½ cup avocado oil mayonnaise
- 2 tablespoons Dijon mustard
- 1 teaspoon dried tarragon or 1 tablespoon chopped fresh tarragon
- Zest and juice of ½ grapefruit (about 2 tablespoons juice)
- ½ teaspoon salt
- ¼ teaspoon freshly ground black pepper
- 1 to 2 tablespoons water (optional)

### DIRECTIONS:
- In a large mason jar or glass measuring cup, combine the mayonnaise, Dijon, tarragon, grapefruit zest and juice, salt, and pepper, and whisk well with a fork until smooth and creamy.
- If a thinner dressing is preferred, thin it out with water.

Per Serving (2 tablespoons): calories: 86 fat: 7g protein: 1g carbs: 6g fiber: 0g sodium: 390mg

## Bagna Cauda

**PREP TIME: 5 MINUTES**
**COOK TIME: 20 MINUTES**
**SERVES 8 TO 10**

### INGREDIENTS:
- ½ cup extra-virgin olive oil
- 4 tablespoons (½ stick) butter (optional)
- 8 anchovy fillets, very finely chopped
- 4 large garlic cloves, finely minced
- ½ teaspoon salt
- ½ teaspoon freshly ground black pepper

### DIRECTIONS:
- In a small saucepan, heat the olive oil and butter (if desired) over medium-low heat until the butter is melted.
- Add the anchovies and garlic and stir to combine. Add the salt and pepper and reduce the heat to low. Cook, stirring occasionally, until the anchovies are very soft and the mixture is very fragrant about 20 minutes.
- Serve warm, drizzled over steamed vegetables as a dipping sauce for raw veggies or cooked artichokes, or use as a salad dressing. Store leftovers in an airtight container in the refrigerator for up to 2 weeks.

Per Serving (2 tablespoons): calories: 181 fat: 20g protein: 1g carbs: 1g fiber: 0g sodium: 333mg

## Olives and Cheese Stuffed Tomatoes

**PREPARATION TIME: 10 MINUTES**
**COOKING TIME: 0 MINUTE**
**SERVINGS: 2**

### INGREDIENTS:
- 24 cherry tomatoes, top cut off, and insides scooped out
- 2 tablespoons olive oil
- ¼ teaspoon red pepper flakes
- ½ cup feta cheese, crumbled
- 2 tablespoons black olive paste
- ¼ cup mint, torn

### DIRECTIONS:
- In a bowl, mix the olives paste with the rest of the ingredients except the cherry tomatoes and whisk well.
- Stuff the cherry tomatoes with this mix, arrange them all on a platter, and serve as an appetizer.

Nutrition: 136 Calories 8.6g Fat 5.6g Carbohydrates 5.1g Protein

## Rosemary Garlic Infused Olive Oil

**PREP TIME: 5 MINUTES**
**COOK TIME: 30 MINUTES**
**MAKES 1 CUP**

### INGREDIENTS:
- 1 cup extra-virgin olive oil
- 4 large garlic cloves, smashed
- 4 (4- to 5-inch) sprigs of rosemary

### DIRECTIONS:
- In a medium skillet, heat the olive oil, garlic, and rosemary sprigs over low heat. Cook until fragrant and garlic is very tender, 30 to 45 minutes, stirring occasionally. Don't let the oil get too hot, or the garlic will burn and become bitter.
- Remove from the heat and allow to cool slightly. Remove the garlic and rosemary with a slotted spoon and pour the oil into a glass container. Allow cooling completely before covering. Store covered at room temperature for up to 3 months.

Per Serving (2 tablespoons): calories: 241 fat: 26g protein: 0g carbs: 1g fiber: 0g sodium: 1mg

## Marinara Sauce

**PREP TIME: 15 MINUTES**
**COOK TIME: 40 MINUTES**
**MAKES 8 CUPS**

### INGREDIENTS:
- 1 small onion, diced
- 1 small red bell pepper, stemmed, seeded, and chopped
- 2 tablespoons plus ¼ cup extra-virgin olive oil, divided
- 2 tablespoons butter (optional)
- 4 to 6 garlic cloves, minced
- 2 teaspoon salt, divided
- ½ teaspoon freshly ground black pepper
- 2 (32-ounce / 907-g) cans of crushed tomatoes (with basil, if possible), with their juices
- ½ cup thinly sliced basil leaves, divided
- 2 tablespoons chopped fresh rosemary
- 1 to 2 teaspoons crushed red pepper flakes (optional)

### DIRECTIONS:
- In a food processor, combine the onion and bell pepper and blend until very finely minced.
- In a large skillet, heat 2 tablespoons of olive oil and the butter (if desired) over medium heat. Add the minced onion and red pepper and sauté until just starting to get tender, about 5 minutes.
- Add the garlic, salt, and pepper and sauté until fragrant, another 1 to 2 minutes.
- Reduce the heat to low and add the tomatoes and their juices, the remaining ¼ cup olive oil, ¼ cup basil, rosemary, and red pepper flakes (if using). Stir to combine, then bring to a simmer and cover. Cook over low heat for 30 to 60 minutes to allow the flavors to blend.
- Add remaining ¼ cup chopped fresh basil after removing from heat, stirring to combine.

Per Serving (1 cup): calories: 256 fat: 20g protein: 4g carbs: 19g fiber: 5g sodium: 803mg

## Spanakopita Dip

**PREP TIME: 15 MINUTES**
**COOK TIME: 14 MINUTES**
**SERVES 2**

### INGREDIENTS:
- Olive oil cooking spray
- 3 tablespoons olive oil, divided
- 2 tablespoons minced white onion
- 2 garlic cloves, minced
- 4 cups fresh spinach
- 4 ounces (113 g) cream cheese, softened
- 4 ounces (113 g) feta cheese, divided
- Zest of 1 lemon
- ¼ teaspoon ground nutmeg
- 1 teaspoon dried dill
- ½ teaspoon salt
- Pita chips, carrot sticks, or sliced bread for serving (optional)

### DIRECTIONS:
- Preheat the air fryer to 360°F (182°C). Coat the inside of a 6-inch ramekin or baking dish with olive oil cooking spray.
- In a large skillet over medium heat, heat 1 tablespoon of the olive oil. Add the onion, then cook for 1 minute.
- Add in the garlic and cook, stirring for 1 minute more.
- Reduce the heat to low and mix in the spinach and water. Let this cook for 2 to 3 minutes, or until the spinach has wilted. Remove the skillet from the heat.
- In a medium bowl, combine the cream cheese, 2 ounces of feta, and the remaining 2 tablespoons of olive oil, along with the lemon zest, nutmeg, dill, and salt. Mix until just combined.
- Add the vegetables to the cheese base and stir until combined.
- Pour the dip mixture into the prepared ramekin and top with the remaining 2 ounces of feta cheese.
- Place the dip into the air fryer basket and cook for 10 minutes, or until heated through and bubbling.
- Serve with pita chips, carrot sticks, or sliced bread.

Nutrition: calories: 550 fat: 52g protein: 14g carbs: 9g fiber: 2g sodium: 113mg

## Harissa Sauce

**PREP TIME: 10 MINUTES**
**COOK TIME: 20 MINUTES**
**MAKES 3 TO 4 CUPS**

### INGREDIENTS:
- 1 large red bell pepper, deseeded, cored, and cut into chunks
- 1 yellow onion, cut into thick rings
- 4 garlic cloves, peeled
- 1 cup vegetable broth
- 2 tablespoons tomato paste
- 1 tablespoon tamari
- 1 teaspoon ground cumin
- 1 tablespoon Hungarian paprika

### DIRECTIONS:
- Preheat the oven to 450°F (235°C). Line a baking sheet with parchment paper.
- Place the bell pepper on the prepared baking sheet, flesh-side up, and space out the onion and garlic around the pepper.
- Roast in the preheated oven for 20 minutes. Transfer to a blender.
- Add the vegetable broth, tomato paste, tamari, cumin, and paprika. Purée until smooth. Served chilled or warm.

Per Serving (¼ cup): calories: 15 fat: 1g protein: 1g carbs: 3g fiber: 1g sodium: 201mg

## Pineapple Salsa

**PREP TIME: 10 MINUTES**
**COOK TIME: 0 MINUTES**
**SERVES 6 TO 8**

### INGREDIENTS:
- 1 pound (454 g) fresh or thawed frozen pineapple, finely diced, juices reserved
- 1 white or red onion, finely diced
- 1 bunch cilantro or mint, leaves only, chopped
- 1 jalapeño, minced (optional)
- Salt, to taste

### DIRECTIONS:
- Stir together the pineapple with its juice, onion, cilantro, and jalapeño (if desired) in a medium bowl. Season with salt to taste and serve.
- The salsa can be refrigerated in an airtight container for up to 2 days.

Nutrition: calories: 55 fat: 0g protein: 1g carbs: 12g fiber: 2g sodium: 20mg

## Yogurt Dip

**DIRECTIONS:**
- Mix the yogurt with the pistachios and the rest of the ingredients, whisk well, divide into small cups and serve with pita chips on the side.

PREPARATION TIME: 10 MINUTES
COOKING TIME: 0 MINUTE
SERVINGS: 2

**INGREDIENTS:**
- 2 cups Greek yogurt
- 2 tablespoons pistachios, toasted and chopped
- A pinch of salt and white pepper
- 2 tablespoons mint, chopped
- 1 tablespoon Kalamata olives, pitted and chopped
- ¼ cup zaatar spice
- ¼ cup pomegranate seeds
- 1/3 cup olive oil

Nutrition: 294 Calories 18g Fat 2g Carbohydrates 10g Protein

## Pepper Tapenade

**DIRECTIONS:**
- In your blender, combine the red peppers with the parmesan and the rest of the ingredients and pulse well.
- Divide into cups and serve as a snack.

PREPARATION TIME: 10 MINUTES
COOKING TIME: 0 MINUTE
SERVINGS: 2

**INGREDIENTS:**
- 7 ounces roasted red peppers, chopped
- ½ cup parmesan, grated
- 1/3 cup parsley, chopped
- 14 ounces canned artichokes, drained and chopped
- 3 tablespoons olive oil
- ¼ cup capers, drained
- 1 and ½ tablespoons lemon juice
- 2 garlic cloves, minced

Nutrition: 200 Calories 5.6g Fat 12.4g Carbohydrates 4.6g Protein

## Tomato Bruschetta

**PREPARATION TIME:** 10 MINUTES
**COOKING TIME:** 10 MINUTES
**SERVINGS:** 2

### DIRECTIONS:
- Situate the baguette slices on a baking sheet lined with parchment paper and grease with cooking spray. Bake for 10 minutes at 400 degrees.
- Combine the tomatoes with the basil and the remaining ingredients, toss well and leave aside for 10 minutes. Divide the tomato mix on each baguette slice, arrange them all on a platter and serve.

### INGREDIENTS:
- 1 baguette, sliced
- 1/3 cup basil, chopped
- 6 tomatoes, cubed
- 2 garlic cloves, minced
- A pinch of salt and black pepper
- 1 teaspoon olive oil
- 1 tablespoon balsamic vinegar
- ½ teaspoon garlic powder
- Cooking spray

Nutrition: 162 Calories 4g Fat 29g Carbohydrates 4g Protein

## Coriander Falafel

**PREPARATION TIME:** 10 MINUTES
**COOKING TIME:** 10 MINUTES
**SERVINGS:** 2

### DIRECTIONS:
- In your food processor, combine the beans with the parsley, onion, and the rest of the ingredients except the oil and the flour, and pulse well. Transfer the mix to a bowl, add the flour, stir well, shape 16 balls out of this mix and flatten them a bit.
- Preheat the pan over medium-high heat, add the falafels, cook them for 5 minutes on both sides, put in paper towels, drain excess grease, arrange them on a platter and serve as an appetizer.

### INGREDIENTS:
- 1 cup canned garbanzo beans
- 1 bunch of parsley leaves
- 1 yellow onion, chopped
- 5 garlic cloves, minced
- 1 teaspoon coriander, ground
- A pinch of salt and black pepper
- ¼ teaspoon cayenne pepper
- ¼ teaspoon baking soda
- ¼ teaspoon cumin powder
- 1 teaspoon lemon juice
- 3 tablespoons tapioca flour
- Olive oil for frying

Nutrition: 122 Calories 6.2g Fat 12.3g Carbohydrates 3.1g Protein

## Carrot Salad

**PREPARATION TIME: 5 MINUTES**
**COOKING TIME: 0 MINUTES**
**SERVINGS: 4**

### INGREDIENTS:
- ¼ tsp chipotle powder
- 1 bunch of scallions, sliced
- 1 cup cherry tomatoes, halved
- 1 large avocado, diced
- 1 tablespoon chili powder
- 1 tablespoon lemon juice
- 2 tbsps. olive oil
- 1 tablespoon lime juice
- 2 cups carrots, spiralized
- Salt, to taste

### DIRECTIONS:
- In a salad bowl, combine avocado, cherry tomatoes, scallion, and spiralized carrots. Set aside.
- In a small bowl, chipotle powder, combine salt, chili powder, olive oil, lemon juice, and lime juice, and whisk well with a fork.
- Pour the dressing into the basin and toss to coat well. Serve and enjoy!

Nutritional values: Calories: 243.6 Kcal, Carbs: 24.6g, Fat: 14.8g, Protein: 3g

## Arugula and Mango

**PREPARATION TIME: 5 MINUTES**
**COOKING TIME: 0 MINUTES**
**SERVINGS: 6**

### INGREDIENTS:
- 2½ cups mangoes, peeled, pitted, and sliced
- 2½ cups avocados, peeled, pitted, and sliced
- 1 red onion, sliced
- 6 cups fresh baby arugula
- ¼ cup fresh mint leaves, chopped
- 2 tbsps. fresh orange juice
- Sea salt, as needed

### DIRECTIONS:
- Place all ingredients in a salad bowl and toss gently.
- Refrigerate until ready to serve.

Nutritional values: Calories: 182 Kcal, Carbs: 18.8g, Fat: 2.6g, Protein: 2.6g

## Cauliflower Tabbouleh

**PREPARATION TIME: 15 MINUTES**
**COOKING TIME: 5 MINUTES**
**SERVINGS: 6**

INGREDIENTS:
- ½ cup chopped Italian parsley
- ½ cup chopped pitted Kalamata olives
- 2 tbsps. minced red onion
- Juice of 1 lemon (about 2 tbsps.)
- 6 tbsps. extra-virgin olive oil, divided
- 4 cups riced cauliflower
- ½ large cucumber, peeled, seeded, and chopped
- ½ cup chopped mint leaves
- 3 garlic cloves, finely minced
- 1½ tsp. salt
- ½ tsp. freshly ground black pepper
- 2 cups baby arugula or spinach leaves
- 2 medium avocados, peeled, pitted, and diced
- 1 cup quartered cherry tomatoes

DIRECTIONS:
- In a large skillet, heat 2 tablespoons of olive oil over medium-high heat. With cauliflower, garlic, salt, and pepper, sauté for 4 minutes. Put everything in a big mixing bowl.
- In a large-size mixing bowl, combine the cucumber, mint, parsley, olives, red onion, lemon juice, and the remaining 4 tablespoons of olive oil. Allow for at least 30 minutes in the refrigerator.
- Before serving, add the arugula, avocado and tomatoes, salt and pepper, and mix well. Enjoy!

Nutritional values: Calories: 235 Kcal, Carbs: 12g, Fat: 21g, Protein: 4g

## Bulgur Salad with Carrots and Almonds

**PREPARATION TIME: 2 HOURS**
**COOKING TIME: 0 MINUTES**
**SERVINGS: 4-6**

INGREDIENTS:
- ⅛ teaspoons cayenne pepper
- ⅓ cup chopped fresh cilantro
- ⅓ cup chopped fresh mint
- ⅓ cup extra-virgin olive oil
- ½ cup sliced almonds, toasted
- ½ tsp ground cumin
- 1 cup water
- 1½ cups medium-grind bulgur, rinsed
- 3 scallions, sliced thin
- 4 carrots, peeled and shredded
- 6 tbsps. lemon juice (2 lemons)
- Salt and pepper

DIRECTIONS:
- In a large bowl, mix bulgur, water, ¼ cup lemon juice, and ¼ tsp salt in a container. Cover, and let sit at room temperature for about 1½ hour until grains are softened and liquid is completely absorbed.
- In another bowl, combine the remaining 2 tbsps. lemon juice, oil, cumin, cayenne, and ½ tsp salt, and whisk well with a fork.
- In the bowl with the bulgur, add carrots, shallots, almonds, mint, and cilantro, and toss gently. Drizzle with the emulsion, adjust salt and pepper and serve.

Nutritional values: Calories: 240 Kcal, Carbs: 54g, Fat: 2g, Protein: 7g

## Cauliflower and Cherry Tomato Salad

PREPARATION TIME: 15 MINUTES
COOKING TIME: 20 MINUTES
SERVINGS: 4

DIRECTIONS:
- Steam the cauliflower for 15-20 minutes.
- In a bowl, mix the lemon juice, cherry tomatoes, cauliflower, and parsley. Season with oil and salt, and mix well. Garnish with pine nuts, and serve.

INGREDIENTS:
- 1 head cauliflower
- 2 tbsps. parsley
- 2 cups cherry tomatoes, halved
- 2 tbsps. lemon juice, fresh
- 2 tbsps. pine nuts

Nutritional values: Calories: 64 Kcal, Fat: 3.3g, Protein: 2.8g Carbs: 12g

## Dandelion and Strawberry

PREPARATION TIME: 10 MINUTES
COOKING TIME: 6 MINUTES
SERVINGS: 2

DIRECTIONS:
- Add the onion, ⅛ teaspoon salt to heated oil, stir and cook for 5 minutes, until the onion is tender and golden brown.
- Meanwhile, in a small bowl, place strawberry slices and drizzle with ½ tablespoon lime juice. Stir well to coat them.
- When the onions have turned golden brown, add the remaining lime juice, stir and let cook for 1 minute.
- Transfer the onions to a large salad bowl. Add the strawberries with their juice, and sprinkle with the remaining salt. Mix well and serve.

INGREDIENTS:
- ½ of onion, peeled, sliced
- 5 strawberries, sliced
- 2 cups dandelion greens, rinsed
- 1 tablespoon key lime juice
- 1 tablespoon grapeseed oil
- ¼ tsp. salt

Nutritional values: Calories: 204 Kcal, Carbs: 10.6g, Fat: 16.1g, Protein: 7g

## Octopus and Radish Salad

PREPARATION TIME: 2 HOURS
COOKING TIME: 1 HOUR 30 MINUTES
SERVINGS: 4

DIRECTIONS:
- Combine the tentacles of the octopus, broth, squid rings, salt, and pepper in a saucepan. Bring to a boil, then lower to low heat and continue to cook for 1 hour and 30 minutes.
- Cut the tentacles into pieces and place them in a basin with the squid rings. Toss in the other ingredients, stir well, and chill for 2 hours before serving.

INGREDIENTS:
- 1 big octopus, cleaned and tentacles separated
- 2 ounces calamari rings
- 3 garlic cloves, minced
- 1 white onion, chopped
- ¾ cup chicken stock
- 2 cups radicchio, sliced
- 2 cups radish, sliced
- 1 cup parsley, chopped
- 1 tablespoon olive oil
- Salt and black pepper to taste

Nutritional values: Calories: 287 Kcal, Carbs: 22g, Fat: 9.9g, Protein: 8.4g

## Citrus Salad

PREPARATION TIME: 5 MINUTES
COOKING TIME: 0 MINUTES
SERVINGS: 2

DIRECTIONS:
- In a large bowl, place the arugula, onion, orange, and avocado and toss gently.
- In a small bowl, combine the oil, salt, cayenne pepper, agave syrup, and lime juice and mix well with a whisk or fork. After that, pour the dressing over the salad and serve.

INGREDIENTS:
- 4 slices of onion
- ½ of avocado, peeled, pitted, sliced
- 4 oz. arugula
- 1 orange, zested, peeled, sliced
- 1 teaspoon agave syrup
- ⅛ tsp. salt
- ⅛ tsp. cayenne pepper
- 2 tbsps. key lime juice
- 2 tbsps. olive oil

Nutritional values: Calories: 265Kcal, Carbs: 11.6g, Fat: 24g, Protein: 3.8g

## Ricotta Stuffed Bell Peppers

**PREP TIME: 10 MINUTES**
**COOK TIME: 20 MINUTES**
**SERVES 4**

### INGREDIENTS:
- 2 red bell peppers
- 1 cup cooked brown rice
- 2 Roma tomatoes, diced
- 1 garlic clove, minced
- ¼ teaspoon salt
- ¼ teaspoon black pepper
- 4 ounces (113 g) ricotta
- 3 tablespoons fresh basil, chopped
- 3 tablespoons fresh oregano, chopped
- ¼ cup shredded Parmesan for topping

### DIRECTIONS:
- Preheat the air fryer to 360°F (182°C).
- Cut the bell peppers in half and remove the seeds and stem.
- In a medium bowl, combine the brown rice, tomatoes, garlic, salt, and pepper.
- Distribute the rice filling evenly among the four bell pepper halves.
- In a small bowl, combine the ricotta, basil, and oregano. Put the herbed cheese over the top of the rice mixture in each bell pepper.
- Place the bell peppers into the air fryer and roast for 20 minutes.
- Remove and serve with shredded Parmesan on top.

Per Serving calories: 156 fat: 6g protein: 8g carbs: 19g fiber: 3g sodium: 264mg

## Roasted Asparagus and Tomatoes

**PREP TIME: 5 MINUTES**
**COOK TIME: 12 MINUTES**
**SERVES 6**

### INGREDIENTS:
- 2 cups grape tomatoes
- 1 bunch asparagus, trimmed
- 2 tablespoons olive oil
- 3 garlic cloves, minced
- ½ teaspoon kosher salt

### DIRECTIONS:
- Preheat the air fryer to 380°F (193°C).
- In a large bowl, combine all of the ingredients, tossing until the vegetables are well coated with oil.
- Pour the vegetable mixture into the air fryer basket and spread into a single layer, then roast for 12 minutes.

Per Serving calories: 57 fat: 5g protein: 1g carbs: 4g fiber: 1g sodium: 197mg

## Spinach Cheese Pies

**PREP TIME: 20 MINUTES**
**COOK TIME: 40 MINUTES**
**SERVES 6 TO 8**

### INGREDIENTS:
- 2 tablespoons extra-virgin olive oil
- 1 large onion, chopped
- 2 cloves garlic, minced
- 3 (1-pound / 454-g) bags of baby spinach, washed
- 1 cup feta cheese
- 1 large egg, beaten
- Puff pastry sheets

### DIRECTIONS:
- Preheat the oven to 375°F (190°C).
- In a large skillet over medium heat, cook the olive oil, onion, and garlic for 3 minutes.
- Add the spinach to the skillet one bag at a time, letting it wilt in between each bag. Toss using tongs. Cook for 4 minutes. Once the spinach is cooked, drain any excess liquid from the pan.
- In a large bowl, combine the feta cheese, egg, and cooked spinach.
- Lay the puff pastry flat on a counter. Cut the pastry into 3-inch squares.
- Place a tablespoon of the spinach mixture in the center of a puff-pastry square. Fold over one corner of the square to the diagonal corner, forming a triangle. Crimp the edges of the pie by pressing down with the tines of a fork to seal them together. Repeat until all squares are filled.
- Place the pies on a parchment-lined baking sheet and bake for 25 to 30 minutes or until golden brown. Serve warm or at room temperature.

Per Serving calories: 503 fat: 32g protein: 16g carbs: 38g fiber: 6g sodium: 843mg

## Ratatouille

**PREP TIME: 15 MINUTES**
**COOK TIME: 40 MINUTES**
**SERVES 6**

### INGREDIENTS:
- 2 russet potatoes, cubed
- ½ cup Roma tomatoes, cubed
- 1 eggplant, cubed
- 1 zucchini, cubed
- 1 red onion, chopped
- 1 red bell pepper, chopped
- 2 garlic cloves, minced
- 1 teaspoon dried mint
- 1 teaspoon dried parsley
- 1 teaspoon dried oregano
- ½ teaspoon salt
- ½ teaspoon black pepper
- ¼ teaspoon red pepper flakes
- ⅓ cup olive oil
- 1 (8-ounce / 227-g) can tomato paste
- ¼ cup vegetable broth
- ¼ cup water

### DIRECTIONS:
- Preheat the air fryer to 320°F (160°C).
- In a large bowl, combine the potatoes, tomatoes, eggplant, zucchini, onion, bell pepper, garlic, mint, parsley, oregano, salt, black pepper, and red pepper flakes.
- In a small bowl, mix together the olive oil, tomato paste, broth, and water.
- Pour the oil-and-tomato-paste mixture over the vegetables and toss until everything is coated.
- Pour the coated vegetables into the air fryer basket in an even layer and roast for 20 minutes. After 20 minutes, stir well and spread out again. Roast for an additional 10 minutes, then repeat the process and cook for another 10 minutes.

Per Serving: calories: 280 fat: 13g protein: 6g carbs: 40g fiber: 7g sodium: 264mg

## Lemon Green Beans with Red Onion

PREP TIME: 5 MINUTES
COOK TIME: 10 MINUTES
SERVES 6

DIRECTIONS:
- Preheat the air fryer to 360°F (182°C). In a large bowl, toss the green beans, onion, olive oil, salt, pepper, and lemon juice until combined.
- Pour the mixture into the air fryer and roast for 5 minutes. Stir well and roast for 5 minutes more.
- Serve with lemon wedges.

INGREDIENTS:
- 1 pound (454 g) of fresh green beans, trimmed
- ½ red onion, sliced
- 2 tablespoons olive oil
- ½ teaspoon salt
- ¼ teaspoon black pepper
- 1 tablespoon lemon juice
- Lemon wedges, for serving

Per Serving: alories: 67 fat: 5g protein: 1g carbs: 6g fiber: 2g sodium: 199mg

## Zucchini with Garlic and Red Pepper

PREP TIME: 5 MINUTES
COOK TIME: 15 MINUTES
SERVES 6

DIRECTIONS:
- Preheat the air fryer to 380°F (193°C).
- In a large bowl, mix together the zucchini, bell pepper, and garlic with olive oil and salt.
- Pour the mixture into the air fryer basket, and roast for 7 minutes. Shake or stir, then roast for 7 to 8 minutes more.

INGREDIENTS:
- 2 medium zucchini, cubed
- 1 red bell pepper, diced
- 2 garlic cloves, sliced
- 2 tablespoons olive oil
- ½ teaspoon salt

Per Serving calories: 57 fat: 5g protein: 1g carbs: 4g fiber: 1g sodium: 197mg

## Carrot and Bean Stuffed Peppers

**PREP TIME: 20 MINUTES**
**COOK TIME: 30 MINUTES**
**SERVES 6**

### INGREDIENTS:
- 6 large bell peppers, different colors
- 3 tablespoons extra-virgin olive oil
- 1 large onion, chopped
- 3 cloves garlic, minced
- 1 carrot, chopped
- 1 (16-ounce / 454-g) can of garbanzo beans, rinsed and drained
- 3 cups cooked rice
- 1½ teaspoons salt
- ½ teaspoon freshly ground black pepper

### DIRECTIONS:
- Preheat the oven to 350°F (180°C).
- Make sure to choose peppers that can stand upright. Cut off the pepper cap and remove the seeds, reserving the cap for later. Stand the peppers in a baking dish.
- In a large skillet over medium heat, cook the olive oil, onion, garlic, and carrots for 3 minutes.
- Stir in the garbanzo beans. Cook for another 3 minutes.
- Remove the pan from the heat and spoon the cooked ingredients into a large bowl.
- Add the rice, salt, and pepper; toss to combine.
- Stuff each pepper to the top and then put the pepper caps back on.
- Cover the baking dish with aluminum foil and bake for 25 minutes.
- Remove the foil and bake for another 5 minutes.
- Serve warm.

Per Serving calories: 301 fat: 9g protein: 8g carbs: 50g fiber: 8g sodium: 597mg

## Garlic Eggplant Slices

**PREP TIME: 5 MINUTES**
**COOK TIME: 25 MINUTES**
**SERVES 4**

### INGREDIENTS:
- 1 egg
- 1 tablespoon water
- ½ cup whole wheat bread crumbs
- 1 teaspoon garlic powder
- ½ teaspoon dried oregano
- ½ teaspoon salt
- ½ teaspoon paprika
- 1 medium eggplant, sliced into ¼-inch-thick rounds
- 1 tablespoon olive oil

### DIRECTIONS:
- Preheat the air fryer to 360°F (182°C).
- In a medium shallow bowl, beat together the egg and water until frothy.
- In a separate medium shallow bowl, mix together bread crumbs, garlic powder, oregano, salt, and paprika.
- Dip each eggplant slice into the egg mixture, then into the bread crumb mixture, coating the outside with crumbs. Place the slices in a single layer at the bottom of the air fryer basket.
- Drizzle the tops of the eggplant slices with the olive oil, then fry for 15 minutes. Turn each slice and cook for an additional 10 minutes.

Per Serving: calories: 137 fat: 5g protein: 5g carbs: 19g fiber: 5g sodium: 409mg

## Roasted Acorn Squash with Sage

PREP TIME: 10 MINUTES COOK TIME: 35 MINUTES SERVES 6

### INGREDIENTS:
- 2 acorn squash, medium to large
- 2 tablespoons extra-virgin olive oil
- 1 teaspoon salt, plus more for seasoning
- 5 tablespoons unsalted butter (optional)
- ¼ cup chopped sage leaves
- 2 tablespoons fresh thyme leaves
- ½ teaspoon freshly ground black pepper

### DIRECTIONS:
- Preheat the oven to 400°F (205°C).
- Cut the acorn squash in half lengthwise. Scrape out the seeds with a spoon and cut them horizontally into ¾-inch-thick slices.
- In a large bowl, drizzle the squash with the olive oil, sprinkle with salt, and toss together to coat.
- Lay the acorn squash flat on a baking sheet.
- Put the baking sheet in the oven and bake the squash for 20 minutes. Flip squash over with a spatula and bake for another 15 minutes.
- Melt the butter (if desired) in a medium saucepan over medium heat.
- Add the sage and thyme to the melted butter and let them cook for 30 seconds.
- Transfer the cooked squash slices to a plate. Spoon the butter/herb mixture over the squash. Season with salt and black pepper. Serve warm.

Per Serving: calories: 188 fat: 15g protein: 1g carbs: 16g fiber: 3g sodium: 393mg

## Savory Sweet Potatoes with Parmesan

PREP TIME: 10 MINUTES
COOK TIME: 18 MINUTES
SERVES 4

### INGREDIENTS:
- 2 large sweet potatoes, peeled and cubed
- ¼ cup olive oil
- 1 teaspoon dried rosemary
- ½ teaspoon salt
- 2 tablespoons shredded Parmesan

### DIRECTIONS:
- Preheat the air fryer to 360°F (182°C).
- In a large bowl, toss the sweet potatoes with olive oil, rosemary, and salt.
- Pour the potatoes into the air fryer basket and roast for 10 minutes, then stir the potatoes and sprinkle the Parmesan over the top. Continue roasting for 8 minutes more.
- Serve hot and enjoy.

Per Serving calories: 186 fat: 14g protein: 2g carbs: 13g fiber: 2g sodium: 369mg

# Stew and Soup Recipes

## Green breakfast soup

**PREPARATION TIME: 8 MINUTES**
**COOKING TIME: 4 MINUTES**
**SERVINGS: 2**

### INGREDIENTS:
- 4 cups of spinach
- 4 cups of vegetable stock
- 2 teaspoons of ground coriander
- One avocado
- Black pepper to taste
- 1 teaspoon of cumin
- 1 teaspoon of turmeric

### DIRECTIONS:
- Put all ingredients in a blender and continue to grind until smooth.
- Transfer the ground mixture to a saucepan and cook until 2-3 minutes. Soup is ready

Nutrition values: Calories: 95Kcal, Protein: 3g, Fat: 3.8g, Carbs: 13.2g

## Creamy broccoli soup

**PREPARATION TIME: 10 MINUTES**
**COOKING TIME: 20 MINUTES**
**SERVINGS: 2 TO 3**

### INGREDIENTS:
- 2 cups of chopped broccoli
- 1 teaspoon of olive oil
- Half roughly chopped sweet onion
- 4 cups of vegetable broth
- ¼ cup of grated parmesan cheese
- Black pepper as per taste
- 1 cup of rice milk

### DIRECTIONS:
- Add the onion to heated olive oil & cook for 3-5 min, until the onion begins to soften. Add broccoli & broth. Season it with pepper.
- Bring a boil & reduce the heat. Then simmer uncovered for 10 min, until broccoli is tendered but bright green.
- Now put the soup mixture into a blender. Add rice milk & process until smooth. Now put in the saucepan, add some parmesan cheese & serve.

Nutrition values: Calories: 243Kcal, Protein: 10.5g, Fat: 12.7g, Carbs: 25.2g

## Roasted tomato basil soup

**PREPARATION TIME: 10 MINUTES**
**COOKING TIME: 50 MINUTES**
**SERVINGS: 2 TO 4**

### INGREDIENTS:
- Three lb. of halved Roma tomatoes
- Olive oil
- Two chopped carrots
- Salt to taste
- Two chopped yellow onions
- Black pepper to taste
- Five minced garlic cloves
- 2 ounces of basil leaves
- 1 cup of crushed tomatoes
- Three thyme sprigs
- 1 teaspoon of dry oregano
- 2 teaspoons of thyme leaves
- ½ teaspoon of paprika
- 2 ½ cups of water
- ½ teaspoon of cumin
- 1 tablespoon of lime juice

### DIRECTIONS:
Mix salt, olive oil, carrot, black pepper, and tomatoes in a bowl.
- Transfer carrot mixture to a baking tray and bake in a preheated oven at 450°F for 30 minutes.
- Blend baked tomato mixture in a blender. You can add little water if needed during blending.
- Sauté onions in heated olive oil over medium flame in a pot for three minutes.
- Mix garlic and cook for one more minute.
- Transfer the blended tomato mixture to the pot, followed by the addition of crushed tomatoes, water, spices, thyme, salt, basil, and pepper.
- Let it boil. Reduce the flame and cook gently for 20 minutes.
- Drizzle lemon juice and serve.

Nutrition values: Calories: 114Kcal, Protein: 4.5g, Fat: 1g, Carbs: 23.7g

## Salmon soup

**PREPARATION TIME: 10 MINUTES**
**COOKING TIME: 13 MINUTES**
**SERVINGS: 2 TO 4**

### INGREDIENTS:
- Olive oil
- Half chopped green bell pepper
- Four chopped green onions
- Four minced garlic cloves
- 5 cups of chicken broth
- One ounce of chopped dill
- One lb. of sliced gold potatoes
- 1 teaspoon of dry oregano
- One sliced carrot
- ¾ teaspoons of coriander
- Kosher salt to taste
- ½ teaspoon of cumin
- Black pepper to taste
- Zest of one lemon
- One lb. of sliced salmon fillet
- 1 tablespoon of lemon juice

### DIRECTIONS:
- Cook onions, garlic, and bell pepper in heated olive oil in a pot over medium flame for four minutes.
- Stir in the dill and cook for half a minute.
- Pour broth into the pot. Add carrot, potatoes, salt, spices, and pepper.
- Let it boil. Reduce the flame and cook gently for six minutes.
- Add salmon and cook for five more minutes.
- Put lemon juice and zest and cook for one minute.
- Serve the soup and enjoy it.

Nutrition values: Calories: 388Kcal, Protein: 32.4g, Fat: 10.7g, Carbs: 30.3g

## Mushroom barley soup

**PREPARATION TIME: 15 MINUTES**
**COOKING TIME: ONE HOUR**
**SERVINGS: 2 TO 4**

### INGREDIENTS:
- Olive oil
- Sixteen ounces of sliced Bella mushrooms
- Kosher salt to taste
- One chopped yellow onion
- Four minced garlic cloves
- Two chopped celery stalks
- One diced carrot
- 8 ounces chopped white mushrooms
- ½ cup of crushed tomatoes
- Black pepper to taste
- 1 teaspoon of coriander
- ½ teaspoon of smoked paprika
- ½ teaspoon of cumin
- 6 cups of broth
- 1 cup of pearl barley
- ½ cup of chopped parsley

### DIRECTIONS:
- Cook mushrooms in heated olive oil over a high flame in a Dutch oven for seven minutes and keep it aside.
- Sauté onions, carrots, white mushrooms, and celery in the same pan with more olive oil for five minutes over medium flame. Sprinkle pepper and salt.
- Stir in tomatoes and spices. Cook for five more minutes.
- Mix barley and broth and boil for five minutes.
- Simmer it for 45 minutes over low flame.
- Add cooked mushrooms and cook for a few more minutes.
- Sprinkle parsley and serve.

Nutrition values: Calories: 198Kcal, Protein: 5.8g, Fat: 9.9g, Carbs: 24g

## Vibrant carrot soup

**PREPARATION TIME: 10 MINUTES**
**COOKING TIME: 25 MINUTES**
**SERVINGS: 2**

### INGREDIENTS:
- 1 tablespoon of olive oil Half chopped onion
- 2 teaspoons of fresh ginger
- 1 teaspoon of fresh minced garlic
- 4 cups of water
- Three chopped carrots
- 1 teaspoon of turmeric powder
- ½ cup of coconut milk
- 1 tablespoon of fresh chopped cilantro

### DIRECTIONS:
- Heat olive oil in a saucepan on medium heat.
- Sauté onion, garlic & ginger till softened for 3 minutes.
- Stir in water, carrots & turmeric. Bring a boil & reduce heat and simmer till the carrots are tendered (20 minutes).
- Transfer soup to a blender along with coconut milk and pulse until soup becomes smooth.
- Serve the soup topped with cilantro.

Nutrition values: Calories: 115Kcal, Protein: 3g, Fat: 11g, Carbs: 9g

## Chilled Pea and mint soup

**PREPARATION TIME: 20 MINUTES**
**COOKING TIME: 25 MINUTES**
**SERVINGS: 2 TO 4**

### INGREDIENTS:
- 2 tablespoons of butter
- One chopped onion medium size
- 2 cups of water
- 2 pounds of frozen green peas
- 2 cups of vegetable broth
- ¼ cup of fresh mint leaves
- ¼ cup of fresh parsley
- 1 teaspoon of fresh lemon juice
- Half teaspoons of cayenne
- Mint leaves for garnishing

### DIRECTIONS:
- Melt the butter in a large pan.
- Add onions & cook till softened for 7 minutes.
- Combine vegetable stock & water in a medium-sized saucepan.
- Stir in ½ of the water mixture in the large pan along with the onions. Increase the heat & bring it to a boil.
- Add peas & bring to a boil for one minute.
- Remove from stove.
- Add the remaining water mixture with the mint, parsley & cayenne.
- Puree with an immersion blender in a pot till it becomes smooth.
- Season using lime juice.
- Cool until chilled.
- Serve in the bowls with mint leaves.

Nutrition values: Calories: 248Kcal, Protein: 8g, Fat: 7g, Carbs: 37g

## Cream of Thyme Tomato Soup

**PREPARATION TIME: 5 MINUTES**
**COOKING TIME: 20 MINUTES**
**SERVINGS: 6**

### INGREDIENTS:
- 2 tbsp ghee
- 2 large red onions, diced
- ½ cup raw cashew nuts, diced
- 2 (28 oz.) cans of tomatoes
- 1 tsp. fresh thyme leaves + extra to garnish
- 1 ½ cups water
- Salt and black pepper to taste

### DIRECTIONS:
- Cook ghee in a pot over medium heat and sauté the onions for 4 minutes until softened.
- Stir in the tomatoes, thyme, water, cashews, and season with salt and black pepper.
- Cover and bring to simmer for 10 minutes until thoroughly cooked.
- Open, turn the heat off, and puree the ingredients with an immersion blender.
- Adjust to taste and stir in the heavy cream.
- Spoon into soup bowls and serve.

Nutrition: 310 Calories 27g Fats 11g Protein

# Cannellini Bean Soup

**PREPARATION TIME: 10 MINUTES**
**COOKING TIME: 20 MINUTES**
**SERVINGS: 2 TO 4**

### INGREDIENTS:
- Two sliced potatoes
- 2 cups of vegetable broth
- Two cans of cannellini beans
- Two diced garlic cloves
- ⅛ teaspoons of black pepper
- ⅓ cup of white wine
- ½ teaspoon of paprika
- ½ teaspoon of salt
- 1 tablespoon of tomato paste
- 1 tablespoon of olive oil
- One sprig rosemary
- One diced onion
- One diced carrot
- 1 cup of spinach
- One diced celery stalk

### DIRECTIONS:
- Heat olive oil over medium heat in a big kettle. Add the diced celery, carrot, and onion until the oil shimmers.
- Cook for about 5 minutes, stirring regularly, till the onion is soft and turns translucent.
- Add the potatoes, tomato paste, beans, garlic, rosemary, and paprika. Cook for about 1 minute, stirring constantly.
- Pour in the wine, mix well, and let it boil for another minute until it has evaporated.
- Then include frozen spinach in the vegetables' broth and a pleasant pinch of salt & pepper. Boost the heat, boil the mixture, gently cover the kettle, reduce the heat and simmer for 15 minutes.
- Remove the pot from heat till the potatoes are soft, and the soup is dense and fluffy, then remove the rosemary sprig—taste and season with pepper and salt. Based on the vegetable broth or your preferences, you can need more salt.
- Break into cups, drizzle with extra virgin olive oil or olive oil, and add more ground black pepper as you prefer. Serve with the crusty wholegrain bread, and add fresh parmesan cheese for extra spice if you do not keep it vegan. Enjoy!

Nutrition values: Calories: 350Kcal, Protein: 19g, Fat: 1g, Carbs: 57g

# Mushroom soup

**PREPARATION TIME: 5 MINUTES**
**COOKING TIME: 45 MINUTES**
**SERVINGS: 2 TO 4**

### INGREDIENTS:
- Salt to taste
- Black pepper to taste
- Six sprigs thyme
- 4 cups of chicken stock
- 3 tablespoons of olive oil
- ¼ cup of whipping cream
- ¼ cup of Cognac
- ¼ cup of chopped chives
- ½ cup of minced shallot
- One sprig rosemary
- One lb. of mixed mushrooms
- One lb. of cremini mushrooms

### DIRECTIONS:
- Chop the mushroom stems roughly and let them simmer, and cover for about an hour in the chicken broth.
- In a large pan, heat oil and sauté each shallot until they are transparent. Lightly add the spices, salt, and pepper.
- Chop the mushroom caps beautifully and precisely into the ½-inch dice. Add them as they are sliced into the shallots. Keep the heat very low until the mushroom fluid is released and then reabsorbed, and cook gently. Shake the cup so that they do not stick. Remove the rosemary and thyme.
- Turn the heat up, then add the Cognac. Flame it up if you. Cook down the mushroom cap or shallot mixture until well reduced and begin to turn the edges a bit golden.
- Strain the fungus from the broth of the chicken.
- To the filtered broth, apply the wonderful shallot mixture and mushroom cap and heat it gently.
- Swirl in and serve the cream and chives. Or serve, if you like to get fancy, in tiny sipping bowls topped with chives and softly whipped cream.

Nutrition values: Calories: 101Kcal, Protein: 11g, Fat: 5g, Carbs: 7g

## Mint avocado chilled soup

**PREPARATION TIME: 10 MINUTES**
**COOKING TIME: 0 MINUTES**
**SERVINGS: 2**

**INGREDIENTS:**
- 1 cup of milk chilled
- 1 tablespoon of lime juice
- Twenty mint leaves
- One ripe avocado
- Two romaine lettuce leaves
- Salt to taste

**DIRECTIONS:**
- Put all ingredients in blender & blend.
- The soup should be dense but not as dense as a puree. Freeze in the fridge for five to ten minutes.
- Serve it.

Nutrition values: Calories: 280Kcal, Protein: 5g, Fat: 26g, Carbs: 12g

## Creamy Cauliflower Soup

**PREPARATION TIME: 15 MINUTES**
**COOKING TIME: 30 MINUTES**
**SERVINGS: 6**

- rice
- 8 oz. cheddar cheese, grated
- 2 cups unsweetened almond milk
- 2 cups vegetable stock
- 2 tbsp water
- 1 small onion, chopped
- 2 garlic cloves, minced
- 1 tbsp olive oil
- Pepper
- Salt

**DIRECTIONS:**
- Cook olive oil in a large stockpot over medium heat.
- Add onion and garlic and cook for 1-2 minutes. Add cauliflower rice and water.
- Cover and cook for 5-7 minutes.
- Now add vegetable stock and almond milk and stir well.
- Bring to boil.
- Turn heat to low and simmer for 5 minutes.
- Turn off the heat.
- Slowly add cheddar cheese and stir until smooth.
- Season soup with pepper and salt.
- Stir well and serve hot.

Nutrition: 214 Calories 16. 5g Fat 11. 6g Protein

## Cauliflower Soup

**PREPARATION TIME: 5 MINUTES**
**COOKING TIME: 20 MINUTES**
**SERVINGS: 4**

### INGREDIENTS:
- 2 cup cauliflower florets, diced
- 1 cup heavy cream
- 2 cup vegetable stock
- 1 tbsp chives, minced
- Salt and pepper to taste
- 1 garlic clove, minced
- 1 tbsp almond butter

### DIRECTIONS:
- In a large saucepan, add the almond butter.
- Toss the garlic until it turns golden.
- Add the cauliflower and toss for 2 minutes.
- Add the vegetable stock and cook on high heat for 10 minutes.
- Add the heavy cream, chives, salt, and pepper, and cook for 8 minutes.
- Serve hot.

Nutrition: 5. 5g Fat 16g Protein 291 Calories

## Easy Cauliflower Soup

**PREPARATION TIME: 5 MINUTES**
**COOKING TIME: 15 MINUTES**
**SERVINGS: 4**

### INGREDIENTS:
- 2 tbsp olive oil
- 2 onions, finely chopped
- 1 tsp. garlic, minced
- 1-pound cauliflower, cut into florets
- 1 cup kale, chopped
- 4 cups vegetable broth
- ½ cup almond milk
- ½ tsp. salt
- ½ tsp. red pepper flakes
- 1 tbsp fresh chopped parsley

### DIRECTIONS:
- Set a pot over medium heat and warm the oil.
- Add garlic and onions and sauté until browned and softened.
- Place in vegetable broth, kale, and cauliflower; cook for 10 minutes until the mixture boils.
- Stir in the pepper flakes, salt, and almond milk; reduce the heat and simmer the soup for 5 minutes.
- Transfer the soup to an immersion blender and blend to achieve the desired consistency; top with parsley and serve immediately.

Nutrition: 172 Calories 10. 3g Fats 8. 1g Protein

## Asparagus Avocado Soup

**PREPARATION TIME: 10 MINUTES**
**COOKING TIME: 20 MINUTES**
**SERVINGS: 4**

### INGREDIENTS:
- 1 avocado, peeled, pitted, cubed
- 12 ounces asparagus
- ½-teaspoon ground black pepper
- 1-teaspoon garlic powder
- 1-teaspoon sea salt
- 2 tablespoons olive oil, divided
- ½ of a lemon, juiced
- 2 cups vegetable stock

### DIRECTIONS:
- Switch on the air fryer, insert the fryer basket, grease it with olive oil, then shut its lid, set the fryer at 425 degrees F, and preheat for 5 minutes.
- Meanwhile, place asparagus in a shallow dish, drizzle with 1-tablespoon oil, sprinkle with garlic powder, salt, and black pepper, and toss until well mixed.
- Open the fryer, add asparagus to it, close with its lid and cook for 10 minutes until nicely golden and roasted, shaking halfway through the frying.
- When the air fryer beeps, open its lid and transfer asparagus to a food processor.
- Add remaining ingredients into a food processor and pulse until well combined and smooth.
- Tip the soup in a saucepan, pour in water if the soup is too thick, and heat it over medium-low heat for 5 minutes until thoroughly heated.
- Ladle soup into bowls and serve.

Nutrition: 208 Calories 11g Fat 4g Protein

## Minty Lentil and Spinach Soup

**PREPARATION TIME: 10 MINUTES**
**COOKING TIME: 30 MINUTES**
**SERVINGS: 6**

### INGREDIENTS:
- 2 tbsp. olive oil
- 1 yellow onion, chopped
- A pinch of salt and black pepper
- 2 garlic cloves, minced
- 1 tsp. coriander, ground
- 1 tsp. cumin, ground
- 1 tsp. sumac
- 1 tsp. red pepper, crushed
- 2 tsp. mint, dried
- 1 tbsp. flour
- 6 cups veggie stock
- 3 cups water
- 12 oz. spinach, torn
- 1 and ½ cups brown lentils, rinsed
- 2 cups parsley, chopped
- Juice of 1 lime

### DIRECTIONS:
- Heat up a pot with the oil over medium heat, add the onions, stir and sauté for 5 minutes.
- Add garlic, salt, pepper, coriander, cumin, sumac, red pepper, mint, and flour, stir and cook for another minute.
- Add the stock, water, and the other ingredients except for the parsley and lime juice, stir, bring to a simmer and cook for 20 minutes.
- Add the parsley and lime juice, cook the soup for 5 minutes more, ladle into bowls and serve.

Nutrition: Calories 170, Fat 7g, Fiber 6g, Carbs 22g, Protein 8g

## Shrimp Soup

**PREPARATION TIME: 30 MINUTES**
**COOKING TIME: 5 MINUTES**
**SERVINGS: 6**

### INGREDIENTS:
- 1 English cucumber, chopped
- 3 cups tomato juice
- 3 jarred roasted red peppers, chopped
- ½ cup olive oil
- 2 tbsp. sherry vinegar
- 1 tsp. sherry vinegar
- 1 garlic clove, mashed
- 2 baguette slices, cut into cubes, and toasted
- Salt and black pepper to taste
- ½ tsp. cumin, ground
- ¾ lb. shrimp, peeled and deveined
- 1 tsp. thyme, chopped

### DIRECTIONS:
- In a blender, mix cucumber with tomato juice, red peppers, and pulse well; bread, 6 tbsp. oil, 2 tbsp. vinegar, cumin, salt, pepper, and garlic, pulse again, transfer to a bowl, and keep in the fridge for 30 minutes.
- Heat a saucepan with 1 tbsp. oil over high heat, add shrimp, stir and cook for 2 minutes.
- Add thyme, and the rest of the ingredients, cook for 1 minute, and transfer to a plate.
- Divide cold soup into bowls, top with shrimp, and serve. Enjoy!

Nutrition: Calories 230, Fat 7g, Fiber 10g, Carbs 24g, Protein 13g

## Cucumber Soup

**PREPARATION TIME: 10 MINUTES**
**COOKING TIME: 6 MINUTES**
**SERVINGS: 4**

### INGREDIENTS:
- 3 bread slices
- ¼ cup almonds
- 4 tsp. almonds
- 3 cucumbers, peeled and chopped
- 3 garlic cloves, minced
- ½ cup warm water
- 6 scallions, thinly sliced
- ¼ cup white wine vinegar
- 3 tbsp. olive oil
- Salt to taste
- 1 tsp. lemon juice
- ½ cup green grapes, cut in halves

### DIRECTIONS:
- Heat a pan over medium-high heat, add almonds, stir, toast for 5 minutes, transfer to a plate and leave aside.
- Soak bread in warm water for 2 minutes, transfer to a blender, and add almost all the cucumber, salt, the oil, garlic, 5 scallions, lemon juice, vinegar, and half of the almonds, and pulse well.
- Ladle soup into bowls, top with reserved ingredients, and 2 tbsp. grapes and serve.

Nutrition: Calories 200, Fat 12g, Fiber 3g, Carbs 20g, Protein 6g

## Chickpeas, Tomato and Kale Stew

**PREPARATION TIME: 10 MINUTES**
**COOKING TIME: 30 MINUTES**
**SERVINGS: 4**

INGREDIENTS:
- 1 yellow onion, chopped
- 1 tbsp. extra-virgin olive oil
- 2 cups sweet potatoes, peeled and chopped
- 1 ½ tsp. cumin, ground
- 4-inch cinnamon stick
- 14 oz. canned tomatoes, chopped
- 14 oz. canned chickpeas, drained
- 1 ½ tsp. honey
- 6 tbsp. orange juice
- 1 cup water
- Salt and black pepper to taste
- ½ cup green olives pitted
- 2 cups kale leaves, chopped

DIRECTIONS:
- Heat a saucepan with the oil over medium-high heat, add onion, cumin, and cinnamon, stir and cook for 5 minutes.
- Add potatoes and the rest of the ingredients except the kale, stir, cover, reduce heat to medium-low and cook for 15 minutes.
- Add kale, stir, cover again and cook for 10 minutes more. Divide into bowls and serve.

Nutrition: Calories 280, Fat 6g, Fiber 9g, Carbs 53g, Protein 10g

## Shrimp & Arugula Soup

**PREPARATION TIME: 5 MINUTES**
**COOKING TIME: 30 MINUTES**
**SERVINGS: 2**

INGREDIENTS:
- 10 medium-sized shrimp or 5 large prawns, cleaned, deshelled, and deveined
- 1 small red onion, sliced very thinly
- 1 cup arugula
- 1 cup baby kale
- 2 large celery stalks, sliced very thinly
- 5 sprigs of parsley, chopped
- 11 cloves of garlic, minced
- 5 cups of chicken or fish or vegetable stock
- 1 tbsp extra virgin olive oil
- Dash of sea salt
- Dash of pepper

DIRECTIONS:
- Sauté the vegetables (not the kale or arugula yet), in a stockpot, on low heat for about 2 minutes so that they are still tender and still crunchy but not cooked quite yet.
- Add the salt and pepper.
- Clean and chop the shrimp into bite-sized pieces that would be comfortable eating in a soup.
- Then, add the shrimp to the pot, and sauté for 10 more minutes on medium-low heat.
- Make sure the shrimp is cooked thoroughly and is not translucent.
- When the shrimp seems to be cooked through, add the stock to the pot and cook on medium for about 20 more minutes.
- Remove from heat and cool before serving.

Nutrition: 254 Calories 2g Fat, 33g Protein

## Creamy Chicken Soup

**PREPARATION TIME:** 10 MINUTES
**COOKING TIME:** 30 MINUTES
**SERVINGS:** 2

### INGREDIENTS:
- 4 chicken breasts
- 1 carrot, chopped
- 1 cup zucchini, peeled and chopped
- 2 cups cauliflower, broken into florets
- 1 celery rib, chopped
- 1 small onion, chopped
- 5 cups water
- ½ tsp salt
- Black pepper, to taste

### DIRECTIONS:
- Place chicken breasts, onion, carrot, celery, cauliflower, and zucchini in a deep soup pot.
- Add in salt, black pepper, and 5 cups of water.
- Stir and bring to a boil.
- Simmer for 30 minutes, then remove the chicken from the pot and let it cool slightly.
- Blend the soup until completely smooth.
- Shred or dice the chicken meat, return it back to the pot, stir, and serve.

Nutrition: 190 Calories 2g Fat 6g Protein

## Easy Tzatziki Sauce

**PREP TIME:** 5 MINUTES
**COOK TIME:** 0 MINUTES
**SERVES 2**

### INGREDIENTS:
- 1 medium cucumber, peeled, seeded, and diced
- ½ teaspoon salt, divided, plus more
- ½ cup plain, unsweetened, full-fat Greek yogurt
- ½ lemon, juiced
- 1 tablespoon chopped fresh parsley
- ½ teaspoon dried minced garlic
- ½ teaspoon dried dill
- Freshly ground black pepper, to taste

### DIRECTIONS:
- Put the cucumber in a colander. Sprinkle with ¼ teaspoon of salt and toss. Let the cucumber rest at room temperature in the colander for 30 minutes.
- Rinse the cucumber in cool water and place it in a single layer on several layers of paper towels to remove the excess liquid.
- In a food processor, pulse the cucumber to chop finely and drain off any extra fluid.
- Pour bthe cucumber into a mixing bowl and add the yogurt, lemon juice, parsley, garlic, dill, and the remaining ¼ teaspoon of salt. Season with salt and pepper to taste, and whisk the ingredients together. Refrigerate in an airtight container.

Nutrition: calories: 77 fat: 3g protein: 6g carbs: 6g fiber: 1g sodium: 607mg

# Beans, Rice, and Grains

## Herbed Risotto

**PREPARATION TIME: 15 MINUTES**
**COOKING TIME: 20 MINUTES**
**SERVINGS: 4**

### INGREDIENTS:
- 2 cups of rice
- 2 tablespoon parmesan cheese, grated
- 3½ ounces heavy cream
- 1 tablespoon fresh oregano, chopped
- 1 tablespoon fresh basil, chopped
- ½ tablespoon fresh sage, chopped
- 1 onion, chopped
- 2 tablespoons olive oil
- 1 teaspoon garlic, minced
- 4 cups vegetable stock
- Salt and black pepper to taste

### DIRECTIONS:
- Add the oil to an Instant Pot and set the pot to Sauté mode.
- Put in garlic and onion and sauté for 2–3 minutes.
- Add remaining ingredients, excluding parmesan cheese and heavy cream, and stir well.
- Seal the pot with the lid and cook on High for 12 minutes.
- Once done, allow to release the pressure naturally for 10 minutes. Then release the remaining pressure using quick release.
- Remove the lid and serve.

Nutrition values: Calories: 514 Kcal, Fat: 17.6g, Carbs: 79.4g, Protein: 8.8g

## Tomato and Millet Mix

**PREPARATION TIME: 10 MINUTES**
**COOKING TIME: 20 MINUTES**
**SERVINGS: 6**

### INGREDIENTS:
- 3 tablespoons olive oil
- 1 cup millet
- 2 scallions, chopped
- 2 tomatoes, chopped
- ½ cup cilantro, chopped
- 1 teaspoon chili paste
- 6 cups of cold water
- ½ cup lemon juice
- Salt and black pepper to taste

### DIRECTIONS:
- Heat a pan with oil over average heat, add the millet, stir, and cook for 4 minutes.
- Add the water, salt, and pepper, stir, and bring to a simmer over medium heat—Cook for 15 minutes.
- Add remaining ingredients and toss well.
- Divide the mixture between plates and serve as a side dish.

Nutrition: Calories: 222 Kcal, Fat: 10.2g, Carbs: 14.5g, Protein: 2.4g

## Fava Beans With Basmati Rice

**PREPARATION TIME: 10 MINUTES**
**COOKING TIME: 35 MINUTES**
**SERVINGS: 4**

### INGREDIENTS:
- ¼ cup olive oil
- 4 cups fresh fava beans, shelled
- 4½ cups water, plus more for drizzling
- 2 cups basmati rice
- ⅛ teaspoon salt
- ⅛ teaspoon freshly ground black pepper
- 2 tablespoons pine nuts, toasted
- ½ cup fresh garlic chives or fresh chives chopped

### DIRECTIONS:
- Fill the saucepan with olive oil and cook over medium heat.
- Add the fava beans and drizzle them with water to avoid them burning or sticking—Cook for 10 minutes.
- Gently stir in the rice. Add the water, salt, and pepper. Increase heat and boil the mixture.
- Lower the heat and simmer for 15 minutes.
- Take away from heat and let it rest for 10 minutes before serving. Spoon onto a serving platter

Nutrition values: Calories: 587 Kcal, Fat: 17g, Carbs: 97g, Protein: 2g

## Mediterranean Spiced Lentils

**PREPARATION TIME: 5 MINUTES**
**COOKING TIME: 20 MINUTES**
**SERVINGS: 6**

### INGREDIENTS:
- 1 teaspoon dried oregano
- ¾ cup green lentils
- 1 teaspoon dried basil
- ¼ teaspoon ground sage
- 2¼ cups water
- ½ teaspoon dried parsley
- ¼ teaspoon onion powder

### DIRECTIONS:
- In a heavy saucepan placed over medium-high heat, add the lentils, water, and spices.
- Let the ingredients come to a boil, and then cover with a lid.
- Reduce heat and simmer for about 20 minutes.
- Stir well and serve hot.

Nutrition values: Calories: 258 Kcal, Fat: 0.9g, Carbs: 44.1g, Protein: 18.7g

# Lentils in Tomato Sauce

PREPARATION TIME: 10 MINUTES
COOKING TIME: 30 MINUTES
SERVINGS: 4

### INGREDIENTS:
- 2½ cups water
- 1 cup green lentils
- 1 tablespoon olive oil
- 1 zucchini, cubed
- ½ large onion, diced
- 2 cloves garlic, minced
- 2 tablespoons lovage, chopped
- 1 tablespoon fresh thyme, chopped
- 2 cups tomato sauce

### DIRECTIONS:
- Add the water to a saucepan, add the lentils, and bring to a boil. Cover and simmer till the lentils are tender (about 20 minutes).
- Heat olive oil in a pan over high heat. Sauté the onion, garlic, and zucchini for 5–7 minutes.
- Add the lovage and thyme and cook until slightly wilted (about 10 seconds).
- Add the lentils and tomato sauce.
- Reduce the heat and cook for 3–5 minutes.

Nutrition values: Calories: 288 Kcal, Fat: 10.5g, Carbs: 39g, Protein: 11g

# Greek Inspired Rice

PREPARATION TIME: 10 MINUTES
COOKING TIME: 30 MINUTES
SERVINGS: 4

### INGREDIENTS:
- 1 yellow onion, chopped
- 1 cup fresh parsley, chopped
- 1 teaspoon dill weed
- 2 cups rice
- 1 garlic clove, minced
- 2 ounces spinach
- ½ cup orzo pasta
- 3 tablespoons olive oil
- 2 tablespoons lemon juice
- 2 cups broth
- A pinch of salt

### DIRECTIONS:
- Wash and leave rice in cold water for 20 minutes. Drain.
- Heat oil in a pan over average heat. Put onion and garlic and cook for 3–4 minutes.
- Add the pasta and cook until it gains some color. Now add the rice.
- Add the spinach, lemon juice, and broth. Boil and lower heat to medium.
- Cover the pot and cook till the rice is done (around 20 minutes). All liquid should be completely absorbed and the rice tender. Remove from the heat.
- For better flavor, leave the pot covered, and don't stir the rice (about 10 minutes).
- Uncover and stir in the parsley and lemon zest.
- Serve and enjoy.

Nutrition values: Calories: 145 Kcal, Fat: 6.9g, Carbs: 18.3g, Protein: 3.3g

# Herbed Rice

**PREPARATION TIME: 10 MINUTES**
**COOKING TIME: 20 MINUTES**
**SERVINGS: 4**

### INGREDIENTS:
- 1 teaspoon salt
- 2 tablespoons olive oil
- 1 onion, chopped
- 1 teaspoon black pepper
- 3 cups chicken broth
- 1 teaspoon garlic, minced
- ¼ cup lemon juice
- ½ cup basmati rice
- ½ teaspoon each of dried rosemary, basil, dill, parsley, oregano, and thyme

### DIRECTIONS:
- Melt the olive oil in a pan on moderate heat. Add the salt and black pepper.
- Add onion and cook till softened. Add garlic and cook for 1 minute.
- Add the chicken broth and lemon juice, along with the dried herbs and rice. Keep stirring until mixed.
- Wait for the mixture to boil, then cover and lower the heat.
- Keep cooking until the rice is well softened.
- Serve and enjoy.

Nutrition values: Calories: 227 Kcal, Fat: 0g, Carbs: 49g, Protein: 4g

# Rice and Veggie Jambalaya

**PREPARATION TIME: 20 MINUTES**
**COOKING TIME: 55 MINUTES**
**SERVINGS: 4**

### INGREDIENTS:
- 2 tablespoons olive oil
- 2 celery stalks, chopped
- ½ red bell pepper, seeded and chopped
- 1 (14-ounce) can of crushed tomatoes (low-sodium)
- 4 cups low-sodium vegetable broth
- 2 tablespoons low-sodium soy sauce
- 1 teaspoon dried thyme, crushed
- 1 teaspoon dried oregano, crushed
- ½ teaspoon smoked paprika
- Salt and black pepper to taste
- 1 scallion, chopped
- 1 onion, chopped
- 4 garlic cloves, minced
- ½ green bell pepper, seeded and chopped
- 2 cups brown rice, uncooked
- 2 tablespoons Tabasco sauce
- 2 bay leaves
- 1 teaspoon dried basil, crushed
- 1 teaspoon sweet paprika
- ½ teaspoon cayenne pepper
- 3 cups canned low-sodium mixed beans (chickpeas, white beans, and kidney beans)

### DIRECTIONS:
- In a large pan placed over average heat, sauté the olive oil, onion, and garlic for about 5 minutes.
- Add the celery and bell peppers and sauté for about 5 minutes.
- Stir in the crushed tomatoes, broth, rice, Tabasco sauce, bay leaves, soy sauce, dried herbs, spices, and black pepper, and let boil.
- Lower the heat, cover the pan, and simmer for about 40 minutes, occasionally stirring, until the rice is cooked.
- Uncover the lid and stir in the beans and salt.
- Simmer for about 3 minutes until heated through.
- Reduce the heat and serve garnished with the scallions.

Nutrition values: Calories: 518 Kcal, Fat: 11.2g, Carbs: 89g, Protein: 16g

## Quinoa, Bean, and Vegetable Stew

**PREPARATION TIME: 20 MINUTES**
**COOKING TIME: 45 MINUTES**
**SERVINGS: 6**

### INGREDIENTS:
- 2 cups seasonal vegetables (zucchini, yellow squash, bell pepper, sweet potatoes), chopped
- 3 tablespoons olive oil, extra-virgin
- 3 carrots, peeled and chopped
- 1 medium yellow onion, chopped
- 6 garlic cloves, minced
- 1 (28-ounce) can of diced tomatoes with juices (low-sodium)
- 4 cups low-sodium vegetable broth
- 2 bay leaves
- Salt and black pepper to taste
- 1 cup fresh kale, chopped
- ¼ cup parmesan cheese, freshly grated
- 2 celery stalks, chopped
- ½ teaspoon dried thyme, crushed
- 1 cup quinoa, rinsed and drained
- 2 cups water
- 1 pinch of red pepper flakes, crushed
- 1 (15-ounce) can of low-sodium Great Northern beans, rinsed and drained
- 2 teaspoons fresh lemon juice

### DIRECTIONS:
- Put the olive oil, seasonal vegetables, carrots, celery, garlic, thyme, onion, and a pinch of salt in a large wok placed over medium heat. Cook for about 8 minutes, stirring occasionally.
- Mix in diced tomatoes with their juices and cook for about 3 minutes, stirring occasionally.
- Add the quinoa, water, broth, red pepper flakes, bay leaves, 1 teaspoon of salt, and black pepper and stir well.
- High heat and let the mixture boil.
- Lower heat, cover partially and simmer for about 25 minutes.
- Stir in the kale and beans and simmer, uncovered, for about 5 minutes.
- Remove from the heat and dispose of the bay leaves.
- Mix in lemon juice and serve topped with parmesan cheese.

Nutrition values: Calories: 507 Kcal, Fat: 11.9g, Carbs: 76.9g, Protein: 26.9g

## Mediterranean Spinach and Beans

**PREPARATION TIME: 10 MINUTES**
**COOKING TIME: 20 MINUTES**
**SERVINGS: 4**

### INGREDIENTS:
- 1 small onion, chopped
- 1 tablespoon olive oil
- 2 garlic cloves, minced
- 2 tablespoons Worcestershire sauce
- ¼ teaspoon pepper
- 1 can (15 ounces) of cannellini beans, washed and drained
- 8 cups fresh baby spinach
- 1 can (14½-ounces) diced no-salt-added tomatoes, undrained
- ¼ teaspoon salt
- ⅛ teaspoon red pepper flakes, crushed
- 1 can (14 ounces) of water-packed artichoke hearts, rinsed, drained, and quartered

### DIRECTIONS:
- Heat olive oil in a skillet, place on average-high heat and sauté the garlic and onion for about 5 minutes.
- Add the Worcestershire sauce, tomatoes, and seasonings, and let the mixture boil.
- Turn down the heat and simmer for about 6-8 minutes.
- Stir in the beans, spinach, and artichoke hearts, and cook for about 5 minutes.

Nutrition values: Calories: 241 Kcal, Fat: 4.3g, Carbs: 39.5g, Protein: 5.1g

# Cannellini Beans and Farro Stew

**PREPARATION TIME: 20 MINUTES**
**COOKING TIME: 45 MINUTES**
**SERVINGS: 6**

### INGREDIENTS:
- 1 cup carrots, peeled and chopped
- 2 tablespoons olive oil
- 1 cup celery, chopped
- 4 garlic cloves, minced
- 1 cup uncooked farro, rinsed
- 1 bay leaf
- Salt, to taste
- 4 cups fresh kale, chopped
- 1 tablespoon lemon juice, fresh
- 1 cup yellow onion, chopped
- 1 (14½-ounce) can of diced tomatoes
- ½ cup fresh parsley sprigs
- 1 teaspoon dried oregano
- 5 cups low-sodium vegetable broth
- 1 (15-ounce) can of low-sodium cannellini beans, rinsed and drained
- ½ cup feta cheese, crumbled

### DIRECTIONS:
- In a large pan placed over medium-high heat, heat the oil and sauté the celery, carrots, garlic, and onion for about 3 minutes.
- Stir in the farro, tomatoes, parsley sprigs, oregano, bay leaf, broth, and salt, and let boil.
- Lower heat to average low, cover, and simmer for about 20 minutes.
- Discard the parsley sprigs and stir in the kale, cooking for about 15 minutes.
- Stir in cannellini beans and cook for about 5 minutes until thoroughly heated.
- Discard the bay leaf and squeeze in the lemon juice.
- Take away from heat and serve topped with feta cheese.

Nutrition values: Calories: 520 Kcal, Fat: 10.5g, Carbs: 79.1g, Protein: 30g

# Freekeh Pilaf

**PREPARATION TIME: 10 MINUTES**
**COOKING TIME: 1 HOUR 10 MINUTES**
**SERVINGS: 5**

### INGREDIENTS:
- 3¾ cups water
- ¼ cup fresh mint, chopped
- ¼ cup extra-virgin olive oil, with extra for serving
- ¼ cup shelled pistachios, toasted and coarsely chopped
- ¼ teaspoon ground coriander
- ¼ teaspoon ground cumin
- 1 head cauliflower (2 pounds), cored and cut into ½-inch florets
- 1 shallot, minced
- 1½ cups whole freekeh
- 1½ tablespoons lemon juice
- 1½ teaspoons grated fresh ginger
- 3 ounces pitted dates, chopped
- Salt and pepper to taste

### DIRECTIONS:
- Boil water in a pot.
- Put in the freekeh and one tablespoon of salt, return to the boil and cook until the grains are tender (30–45 minutes).
- Drain the freekeh, return to the now-empty pot, and cover to keep warm.
- Warm two tablespoons of oil in a pan on moderate to high heat until it starts to shimmer.
- Put in the cauliflower, salt, and pepper, cover, and cook until the florets are softened and brown, approximately 5 minutes.
- Uncover and continue to cook, stirring intermittently, until the florets turn spotty brown, about 10 minutes.
- Put in the remaining 2 tablespoons of oil, dates, shallot, ginger, coriander, and cumin and cook, often stirring, until the dates and shallot are softened and aromatic, approximately 3 minutes.
- Lower heat, put in the freekeh, and cook, often stirring, until heated through (about 1 minute). Remove from the heat mix in the pistachios, mint, and lemon juice.
- Drizzle with some extra oil.

Nutrition values: Calories: 520 Kcal, Fat: 14g, Carbs: 54g, Protein: 36g

# Brown Rice Pilaf with Raisins

**PREPARATION TIME: 10 MINUTES**
**COOKING TIME: 15 MINUTES**
**SERVINGS: 6**

### INGREDIENTS:
- 1 tablespoon extra-virgin olive oil
- 1 cup onion, chopped
- ½ cup carrot, shredded
- 1 teaspoon ground cumin
- ½ teaspoon ground cinnamon
- 2 cups instant brown rice
- 1¾ cup 100% orange juice
- ¼ cup water
- 1 cup golden raisins
- ½ cup shelled pistachios
- Bunch of fresh chives, chopped (optional)

### DIRECTIONS:
- Heat oil in a medium saucepan.
- Put in onion and simmer, often stirring, for 5 minutes.
- Cook for 1 minute, constantly stirring, after adding the carrot, cumin, and cinnamon.
- Combine the rice, orange juice, and water in a mixing bowl.
- Boil, cover, and reduce to medium-low heat.
- Cook for 7 minutes, or until the rice is tender and the liquid has evaporated.
- Serve with the raisins, pistachios, and chives (if used).

Nutrition values: Calories: 320 Kcal, Fat: 7g, Carbs: 61g Protein: 6g

# Baked Black-Eyed Peas

**PREPARATION TIME: 15 MINUTES**
**COOKING TIME: 35 MINUTES**
**SERVINGS: 3**

### INGREDIENTS:
- 2 (15-ounce) cans of black-eyed peas, drained and rinsed
- 3 tablespoons extra-virgin olive oil
- Salt, to taste
- 2 teaspoons Za'atar
- 2 teaspoons sumac
- 2 teaspoons harissa

### DIRECTIONS:
- Preheat the oven to 400°F.
- Place the black-eyed peas on a baking sheet and drizzle with olive oil.
- Season with salt and toss to coat well.
- Bake for about 35 minutes, shaking the baking pan three times during the cooking time.
- Remove from the oven and season with the Za'atar, sumac, and harissa.
- Serve warm.

Nutrition values: Calories: 478 Kcal, Fat: 18.5g, Carbs: 66.1g, Protein: 14.9g

# Mains

## Chicken Shawarma

**PREPARATION TIME: 8 MINUTES**
**COOKING TIME: 15 MINUTES**
**SERVINGS: 8**

### INGREDIENTS:
- 2 lb. chicken breast, sliced into strips
- 1 teaspoon paprika
- 1 teaspoon ground cumin
- 1/4 teaspoon granulated garlic
- 1/2 teaspoon turmeric
- 1/4 teaspoon ground allspice

### DIRECTIONS
- Season, the chicken with the spices and a little salt and pepper.
- Pour 1 cup of chicken broth into the skillet.
- Seal the skillet.
- Choose a poultry setting.
- Cook for 15 minutes.
- Release the pressure naturally. Serve with flatbread.

Nutrition: 481 calories 21g fats 9g protein

## Turkey and Asparagus Mix

**PREPARATION TIME: 10 MINUTES**
**COOKING TIME: 30 MINUTES**
**SERVINGS: 4**

### INGREDIENTS:
- 1 bunch asparagus, trimmed and halved
- 1 big turkey breast, skinless, boneless, and cut into strips
- 1 teaspoon basil, dried
- 2 tablespoons olive oil
- A pinch of salt and black pepper
- ½ cup tomato sauce
- 1 tablespoon chives, chopped

### DIRECTIONS:
- Heat up a pan with the oil over medium-high heat, add the turkey, and brown for 4 minutes.
- Add the asparagus and the rest of the ingredients except the chives, bring to a simmer and cook over medium heat for 25 minutes.
- Add the chives, divide the mix between plates and serve.

Nutrition: Calories 337, fat 21. 2, fiber 10. 2, carbs 21. 4, protein 17. 6

## Chicken with Olives, Mustard Greens, and Lemon

**PREP TIME: 10 MINUTES**
**COOK TIME: 30 MINUTES**
**SERVINGS 6**

### INGREDIENTS

- 2 tbsp. extra virgin olive oil, divided
- 6 skinless chicken breast halves, cut in half crosswise
- ½ cup Kalamata olives pitted
- 1 tbsp. freshly squeezed lemon juice
- 1 1/2 pounds mustard greens, stalks removed and coarsely chopped
- 1 cup dry white wine
- 4 garlic cloves, smashed
- 1 medium red onion, halved and thinly sliced
- Sea salt
- Ground pepper
- Lemon wedges, for serving

### DIRECTIONS:

- In a Dutch oven or large, heavy pot, heat 1 tablespoon of extra virgin olive oil over medium heat.
- Rub the chicken with sea salt and pepper and add half of it to the mixing bowl; cook on all sides for about 8 minutes or until browned.
- Switch to a plate with the cooked chicken and repeat with the remaining chicken and oil.
- Add the garlic and onion to the pot and heat to medium; cook, stirring, until tender, or about 6 minutes.
- Add the chicken and wine (with accumulated juices) and bring it to a boil.
- Reduce the heat and cook for approximately 5 minutes, sealed.
- On top of the chicken, add the greens and sprinkle it with sea salt and pepper.
- Cook for 5 more minutes or until the greens are wilted and the chicken is opaque.
- Stir in the olives and lemon juice and remove the pot from the heat.
- Serve drizzled and garnished with lemon wedges with the collected pan juices.

Nutrition: Calories 336, fat 20. 2, fiber 12. 2, carbs 22. 4, protein 17. 6

## Chicken with Greek

**PREP TIME: 25 MINUTES**
**COOK TIME: 0 MINUTES**
**SERVING 4**

### INGREDIENTS

- 2 tbsp. extra virgin olive oil
- ⅓ cup red-wine vinegar
- 1 tsp. garlic powder
- 1 tbsp. chopped fresh dill
- ¼ tsp. sea salt
- ¼ tsp. freshly ground pepper
- 2 ½ cups chopped cooked chicken
- 6 cups chopped romaine lettuce
- 1 cucumber, peeled, seeded, and chopped
- 2 medium tomatoes, chopped
- ½ cup crumbled feta cheese
- ½ cup sliced ripe black olives
- ½ cup finely chopped red onion

### INSTRUCTIONS

- Whisk the extra virgin olive oil, vinegar, garlic powder, dill, sea salt, and pepper together in a large cup.
- To combine well, add the chicken, lettuce, cucumber, tomatoes, feta, olives, and toss. Enjoy!

Nutrition: Calories 337, fat 21. 2, fiber 10. 2, carbs 21. 4, protein 17. 6

## Coronation Chicken Salad Sirtfood

**PREPARATION TIME: 2 MINUTES**
**COOKING TIME: 2 MINUTES**
**SERVINGS: 1**

DIRECTIONS:
- Take a bowl, gather the ingredients and mix them in a bowl, and serve the salad on the rocket bedding.

INGREDIENTS:
- 75 g Natural yogurt
- 1 tsp. Coriander, chopped
- Juice of 1/4 of a lemon
- 1/2 tsp. Mild curry powder
- 1 tsp. Ground turmeric
- Walnut halves, finely chopped
- 100 g Cooked chicken breast, cut into bite-sized pieces
- 20 g Red onion, diced
- 1 Bird's eye chili
- 1 Medjool date, finely chopped
- 40 g Rocket, to serve

Nutrition: Calories: 364 Carbs: 45g Fat: 12g Protein: 15g

## Chicken Stuffed Peppers

**PREPARATION TIME: 10 MINUTES**
**COOKING TIME: 0 MINUTES**
**SERVINGS: 6**

DIRECTIONS:
- In a bowl, mix the chicken with the celery and the rest of the ingredients except the bell peppers and toss well.
- Stuff the peppers halves with the chicken mix and serve for lunch.

INGREDIENTS:
- 1 cup Greek yogurt
- tablespoons mustard
- Salt and black pepper to the taste
- 1-pound rotisserie chicken meat, cubed
- 4 celery stalks, chopped
- tablespoons balsamic vinegar
- 1 bunch of scallions, sliced
- ¼ cup parsley, chopped
- 1 cucumber, sliced
- red bell peppers, halved and deseeded
- 1-pint cherry tomatoes, quartered

Nutrition: calories 266, fat 12. 2, fiber 4. 5, carbs 15. 7, protein 3. 7

## Braised Chicken with Mushrooms and Olives

**PREP TIME: 10 MINUTES**
**COOK TIME: 35 MINUTES**
**SERVINGS 4**

### INGREDIENTS
- 2 ½ pounds of chicken, cut into pieces
- Sea salt
- Freshly ground pepper
- 1 tbsp. plus
- 1 tsp. extra virgin olive oil
- 16 cloves garlic, peeled
- 10 ounces cremini mushrooms, rinsed, trimmed, and halved
- ½ cup white wine
- ⅓ cup chicken stock
- ½ cup green olives pitted

### INSTRUCTIONS
- Over medium-high heat, prepare a large skillet.
- Meanwhile, the chicken should be seasoned with sea salt and pepper.
- To the heated skillet, add 1 tablespoon of extra virgin olive oil and add the chicken, skin side down; cook for around 6 minutes or until browned.
- Move it to a dish and set it aside.
- Add 1 teaspoon of the remaining extra virgin olive oil to the pan and sauté for around 6 minutes or until the garlic and mushrooms are browned.
- Add the wine and bring to a boil; reduce the heat and cook for approximately 1 minute.
- Send the chicken back to the pan and stir in the olives and chicken broth. Return the mixture to a gentle boil, reduce heat, and cook, covered, for about 20 minutes or until the chicken is thoroughly cooked.

Nutrition: Calories 437, fat 23. 2, fiber 11. 2, carbs 31. 2, protein 15. 6

## Chicken Skillet

**PREPARATION TIME: 10 MINUTES**
**COOKING TIME: 35 MINUTES**
**SERVINGS: 6**

### INGREDIENTS:
- 6 chicken thighs, bone-in, and skin-on
- Juice of 2 lemons
- 1 teaspoon oregano, dried
- 1 red onion, chopped
- Salt and black pepper to the taste
- 1 teaspoon garlic powder
- 2 garlic cloves, minced
- 2 tablespoons olive oil
- 2 and ½ cups chicken stock
- 1 cup white rice
- 1 tablespoon oregano, chopped
- 1 cup green olives, pitted and sliced
- 1/3 cup parsley, chopped
- ½ cup feta cheese, crumbled

### DIRECTIONS:
- Heat up a pan with the oil over medium heat, add the chicken thighs skin side down, cook for 4 minutes on each side and transfer to a plate.
- Add the garlic and the onion to the pan, stir and sauté for 5 minutes.
- Add the rice, salt, pepper, the stock, oregano, and lemon juice, stir, cook for 1-2 minutes more and take off the heat.
- Add the chicken to the pan, introduce the pan to the oven and bake at 375 degrees F for 25 minutes.
- Add the cheese, olives, and the parsley, divide the whole mix between plates and serve for lunch.

Nutrition: calories 435, fat 18. 5, fiber 13. 6, carbs 27. 8, protein 25. 6

## Chicken and Leeks Pan

**PREPARATION TIME: 10 MINUTES**
**COOKING TIME: 20 MINUTES**
**SERVINGS: 4**

**INGREDIENTS:**
- tablespoons olive oil
- 1 pound chicken breast, skinless, boneless, and cut into strips
- shallots, chopped
- 1 cup mozzarella cheese, shredded
- 2 leeks, sliced
- ½ cup veggie stock
- 1 tablespoon heavy cream
- 1 teaspoon sweet paprika
- Salt and black pepper to the taste

**DIRECTIONS:**
- Ensure that you heat the pan, add the shallots, stir then cook for 3 minutes.
- Add the meat and the leeks, stir and brown for 7 minutes more.
- Add the other ingredients except for the cheese and stir.
- Sprinkle the cheese on top, introduce the pan to the oven, then cook everything at 400 degrees F for 10 minutes more.
- Divide the mix between plates and serve.

Nutrition: calories 253, fat 12. 9, fiber 1, carbs 7. 2, protein 26. 9

## Paprika Chicken Mix

**PREPARATION TIME: 10 MINUTES**
**COOKING TIME: 25 MINUTES**
**SERVINGS: 4**

**INGREDIENTS:**
- 1 cup mozzarella, shredded
- tablespoons olive oil
- shallots, chopped
- 1 pound chicken breast, skinless, boneless, and roughly cubed
- Salt and black pepper to the taste
- 1 cup carrots, sliced
- 1 teaspoon sweet paprika
- ¼ teaspoon onion powder
- ¼ teaspoon garlic powder
- ½ cup chicken stock
- 1 tablespoon chives, chopped

**DIRECTIONS:**
- Ensure that you heat the pan; add the shallots and sauté for 2 minutes.
- Add the carrots, paprika, onion, and garlic powder, stir and sauté for 3 minutes more.
- Add the meat and brown it for 5 minutes more.
- Add the stock, sprinkle the cheese, and then cook everything for 15 minutes more.
- Sprinkle the chives on top, divide the mix between plates and serve.

Nutrition: calories 200, fat 4. 5, fiber 3. 5, carbs 8. 5, protein 10

## Chicken and Peppers Mix

**PREPARATION TIME: 10 MINUTES**
**COOKING TIME: 25 MINUTES**
**SERVINGS: 4**

### INGREDIENTS:
- 1 cup red bell peppers, cut into strips
- 1 pound chicken breast, skinless, boneless, and roughly cubed
- spring onions, chopped
- tablespoons olive oil
- 1 tomato, cubed
- Salt and black pepper to the taste
- ¼ cup tomato passata
- 1 tablespoon cilantro, chopped

### DIRECTIONS:
- Ensure that you heat the pan, add the spring onions, and sauté them for 2 minutes.
- Add the chicken and the bell peppers, stir, then cook everything for 8 minutes more.
- Add the rest of the ingredients, bring to a simmer, then cook over medium heat for 15 minutes more, stirring often.
- Divide the mix between plates and serve

Nutrition: calories 206, fat 10, fiber 0. 9, carbs 3. 7, protein 24. 8

## Honey Balsamic Chicken

**PREPARATION TIME: 7 MINUTES**
**COOKING TIME: 30 MINUTES**
**SERVINGS: 5**

### INGREDIENTS:
- 1/4 cup honey
- 1/2 cup balsamic vinegar
- 1/4 cup soy sauce
- cloves garlic minced
- 10 chicken drumsticks

### DIRECTIONS
- Mix the honey, vinegar, soy sauce, and garlic in a bowl.
- Soak the chicken in the sauce for 30 minutes.
- Cover the skillet.
- Set it to manual.
- Cook at high pressure for 10 minutes.
- Release the pressure quickly.
- Choose the sauté button to thicken the sauce.

Nutrition: 517 calories 26g fats 10g protein

## Garlic and Lemon Chicken Dish

**PREPARATION TIME: 11 MINUTES**
**COOKING TIME: 10 MINUTES**
**SERVINGS: 4**

### INGREDIENTS
- 2-3 pounds of chicken breast
- 1 teaspoon salt
- 1 onion, diced
- 1 tablespoon ghee
- garlic cloves, minced
- ½ cup organic chicken broth
- 1 teaspoon dried parsley
- 1 large lemon, juiced
- 3-4 teaspoon arrowroot flour

### DIRECTIONS
- Set your skillet to Sauté mode. Add diced up onion and cooking fat
- Allow the onions to cook for 5-10 minutes
- Add the rest of the ingredients except arrowroot flour
- Lock up the lid and set the skillet to poultry mode. Cook until the timer runs out
- Allow the pressure to release naturally
- Once done, remove ¼ cup of the sauce from the skillet and add arrowroot to make a slurry
- Add the slurry to the skillet to make the gravy thick. Keep stirring well. Serve!

Nutrition: 511 calories 29g fats 11g protein

## Warm Chicken Avocado Salad

**PREP TIME: 15 MINUTES**
**COOK TIME: 20 MINUTES**
**SERVINGS 4**

### INGREDIENTS
- 2 tbsp. extra virgin olive oil, divided
- 500g chicken breast fillets
- 1 large avocado, peeled, diced
- 2 garlic cloves, sliced
- 1 tsp. ground turmeric
- 3 tsp. ground cumin
- 1 small head of broccoli, chopped
- 1 large carrot, diced
- 1/3 cup currants
- 1 1/2 cups chicken stock
- 1 1/2 cups couscous
- Pinch of sea salt

### INSTRUCTIONS
- Heat 1 tablespoon of extra virgin olive oil in a large frying pan set over medium heat; add chicken and cook for about 6 minutes on each side or until cooked through; move to a plate and keep warm.
- Meanwhile, in a heatproof dish, mix the currants and couscous; stir in the boiling stock and set aside, covered, for at least 5 minutes or until the liquid has been absorbed.
- Separate the grains with a fork.
- In a frying pan, add the remaining oil and add carrots; cook for about 1 minute, stirring.
- For about 1 minute, stir in the broccoli; add the garlic, turmeric, and cumin.
- Cook for another 1 minute or so, then remove the pan from the oven.
- Break the chicken into small slices and add to the mixture of broccoli; toss to combine; season with sea salt, and serve with the sprinkled avocado on top.

Nutrition: Calories 327, fat 21.2, fiber 13.2, carbs 20.4, protein 17.6

## Belizean Chicken Stew

**PREPARATION TIME: 7 MINUTES**
**COOKING TIME: 23 MINUTES**
**SERVINGS: 4**

### INGREDIENTS
- whole chicken
- 1 tablespoon coconut oil
- tablespoons achiote seasoning
- tablespoons white vinegar
- tablespoons Worcestershire sauce
- 1 cup yellow onion, sliced
- garlic cloves, sliced
- 1 teaspoon ground cumin
- 1 teaspoon dried oregano
- ½ teaspoon black pepper
- cups chicken stock

### DIRECTIONS
- Take a large-sized bowl and add achiote paste, vinegar, Worcestershire sauce, oregano, cumin, and pepper. Mix well and add chicken pieces and rub the marinade all over them
- Allow the chicken to sit overnight. Set your skillet to Sauté mode and add coconut oil
- Once hot, cook chicken pieces in the skillet in batches. Remove the seared chicken and transfer them to a plate
- Add onions and garlic to the skillet and Sauté for 2-3 minutes. Add chicken pieces back to the skillet
- Pour chicken broth into the bowl with marinade and stir well. Add the mixture to the skillet
- Seal up the lid and cook for about 20 minutes at high pressure
- Once done, release the pressure naturally. Season with a bit of salt, and serve!

Nutrition: 517 calories 21g fats 9g protein

## Pistachio-Crusted Halibut

**PREPARATION TIME: 15 MINUTES**
**COOKING TIME: 20 MINUTES**
**SERVINGS: 4**

### INGREDIENTS:
- 4 (6-Oz) Halibut Fillets with Skin Removed.
- ½ Cup Shelled Unsalted Pistachios (Chopped).
- 4 tsp. Fresh Parsley (Chopped).
- 1 Cup Bread Crumbs.
- ¼ Cup Extra-Virgin Olive Oil.
- 2 tsp. Grated Orange Zest.
- 1 Tsp. Grated Lime Zest.
- ½ Tsp. Pepper.
- 4 tsp. of Dijon Mustard.
- 1 1/2 of Salt.

### DIRECTIONS:
- Preheat the oven to 4000F.
- In the food processor, add pistachio, zest, bread crumbs, parsley, and oil. Pulse until the ingredients are well combined.
- Rinse the fish and pat dry with a paper towel. Season the fillet with salt and pepper.
- Brush the fish with mustard and divide the pistachio mix evenly with some on top of the fish. Press down the mixture to allow the crust to adhere.
- Lining the baking sheet with crusted paper, arrange the crusted fish, and bake for 20 minutes or until the fillet is golden brown. Leave for 5 minutes to cool, and then serve.

Nutrition: Calories: 231 Carbs: 31. 5g Protein: 5. 8g Fat: 9. 50g

# Kids Friendly Recipes

## Potato And Chickpea Hash

**PREP TIME: 5 MINUTES**
**COOK TIME: 7 MINUTES**
**SERVINGS: 4**

### INGREDIENTS:
- cups shredded frozen hash brown potatoes
- 1 tbsp. freshly minced ginger
- ½ mug of chopped onion
- cups chopped baby spinach
- 1 tbsp. Curry powder
- ½ tsp. sea salt
- ¼ mug olive oil
- 1 mug of chopped zucchini
- 1 (15-ounce) chickpeas, rinsed
- large eggs

### DIRECTIONS:
- In a large container, combine the potatoes, ginger, onion, spinach, curry powder, and sea salt.
- In a nonstick skillet set over medium to high heat, add olive oil and the potato mixture.
- Press the batter into a layer and cook for about 5 mins, without stirring, or until golden brown and crispy.
- Lower flame to medium-low and fold in zucchini and chickpeas, breaking up the batter until just combined.
- Stir briefly, press the batter back into a layer, and make four wells.
- Break one egg into each indentation.
- Cook it for about 5 mins or until eggs are set.

Nutrition: Calories: 256 Cal Fat: 3.6 g Carbs: 27.2 g Protein: 4.2 g Fiber: 10.2 g

## Creamy Panini

**PREP TIME: 5 MINUTES**
**COOK TIME: 12 MINUTES**
**SERVINGS: 4**

### INGREDIENTS:
- ¼ mug of chopped basil leaves
- ½ mug mayonnaise dressing with Olive Oil divided into eight slices of whole-wheat bread four slices of bacon
- 1 zucchini, thinly sliced
- slices provolone cheese
- oz. roasted red peppers, sliced

### DIRECTIONS:
- In a container, combine olives, basil, and ¼ mug of mayonnaise; evenly spread the mayonnaise batter on the bread slices and layer 4 slices with bacon, zucchini, provolone, and peppers.
- Top it with some bread slices and spread the remaining ¼ mug of mayonnaise on the outside of the sandwiches; cook over medium flame for about 4 mins, turning once, until cheese is melted & the sandwiches get golden brown.

Nutrition: Calories: 278 Cal Fat: 5.6 g Carbs: 37.2 g Protein: 6.2 g Fiber: 13.2 g

## Avocado Toast

**PREP TIME: 5 MINUTES**
**COOK TIME: 12 MINUTES**
**SERVINGS: 4**

### INGREDIENTS:
- ripe avocados, peeled
- A squeeze of lemon juice to taste
- tbsp. freshly chopped mint, plus extra to garnish. Sea salt and black pepper, to taste
- large slices of rye bread
- 80 grams soft feta, crumbled

### DIRECTIONS:
- In a medium container, mash the avocado roughly with a fork; add lemon juice and mint and continue mashing until combined—season with black pepper and salt to taste.
- Grill or toast bread until golden.
- Spread about ¼ of the avocado batter onto each slice of the toasted bread and top with feta.
- Garnish with extra mint and serve immediately.

Nutrition: Calories: 208 Cal Fat: 5.4 g Carbs: 38 g Protein: 6 g Fiber: 8.2 g

## Breakfast Couscous

**PREP TIME: 5 MINUTES**
**COOK TIME: 6 MINUTES**
**SERVINGS: 2**

### INGREDIENTS:
- 1 (2-inch) cinnamon stick
- cups 1% low-fat milk
- 1 mug of whole-wheat couscous (uncooked
- tsp. dark brown sugar, divided
- ¼ mug of dried currants
- ½ mug of chopped apricots (dried)
- ¼ tsp. sea salt
- tsp. melted butter, divided

### DIRECTIONS:
- Place a saucepan on the burner. Keep heat medium to high. Combine cinnamon stick and milk; flame for about 3 mins (do not boil).
- Transfer the pan from flame and stir in couscous, 4 teaspoons of sugar, currants, apricots, and sea salt. Cover the batter and stand it for at least 15 mins.
- Discard the cinnamon stick and divide the couscous among four containers; top each serving with ½ teaspoon of sugar and 1 teaspoon of melted butter. Serve immediately.

Nutrition: Calories: 200 Cal Fat: 4.6 g Carbs: 25.2 g Protein: 5.2 g Fiber: 13.2 g

## Garlicky Scrambled Eggs

PREP TIME: 5 MINUTES
COOK TIME: 24 MINUTES
SERVINGS: 4

### INGREDIENTS:
- ½ tsp. Olive oil
- ½ mug of ground beef
- ½ tsp. garlic powder
- eggs
- Salt
- Pepper

### DIRECTIONS:
- Set a medium-sized pan over medium heat.
- Add olive oil and flame until hot but not smoking.
- Stir in ground beef and cook for about 10 mins or until almost done.
- Stir in garlic and sauté for about 2 mins.
- In a large container, beat the eggs until almost frothy; season with salt and pepper.
- Add the egg batter to the pan with the cooked beef and scramble until ready.
- Serve with toasted bread and olives for a healthy, satisfying breakfast!

Nutrition: Calories: 278 Cal Fat: 5.6 g Carbs: 37.2 g Protein: 6.2 g Fiber: 13.2 g

## Mediterranean Frittata

PREP TIME: 5 MINUTES
COOK TIME: 7 MINUTES
SERVINGS: 6

### INGREDIENTS:
- tbsp. olive oil, divided
- 1 mug of chopped onion
- cloves garlic, minced
- eggs, beaten
- ¼ mug half-and-half, milk or light cream
- ½ mug of sliced Kalamata olives
- ½ mug roasted red sweet peppers, chopped ½ mug crumbled feta cheese ⅛ tsp. black pepper
- ¼ cup basil
- 2 tbsp. Parmesan cheese, finely shredded
- ½ mug of coarsely crushed onion-and-garlic leaves to garnish

### DIRECTIONS:
- Preflame your broiler.
- Flame 2 tbsps of olive oil in a broiler-proof skillet set over medium heat; sauté onion and garlic for a few mins or until tender.
- In the meantime, beat eggs and half-and-half in a container until well combined. Stir in olives, roasted sweet pepper, feta cheese, black pepper, and basil. Pour the egg batter over the sautéed onion batter and cook until almost set.
- With a spatula, lift the egg batter to allow the uncooked part to flow underneath.
- Continue cooking for 2 mins more or until it the set.
- Combine the remaining olive oil, Parmesan cheese, and crushed croutons in a container; sprinkle the batter over the frittata and broil for about 5 mins or until the crumbs are golden and the top is set.
- Garnish with basil and serve.

Nutrition: Calories: 278 Cal Fat: 5.6 g Carbs: 37.2 g Protein: 6.2 g Fiber: 13.2 g

## Banana Shake Bowls

**PREPARATION TIME: 5 MINUTES**
**COOKING TIME: 0 MINUTES**
**SERVINGS: 4**

### INGREDIENTS:
- medium bananas, peeled
- 1 avocado, peeled, pitted, and mashed
- ¾ cup almond milk
- ½ tsp. vanilla extract

### DIRECTIONS:
- In a blender, combine the bananas with the avocado and the other ingredients, pulse, divide into bowls and keep in the fridge until serving.

Nutrition: Calories 185 Fat 4. 3g Carbs 6g Protein 6. 45g

## Cold Lemon Squares

**PREPARATION TIME: 30 MINUTES**
**COOKING TIME: 0 MINUTES**
**SERVINGS: 4**

### INGREDIENTS:
- 1 cup avocado oil, a drizzle
- bananas, peeled and chopped
- 1 tbsp. honey
- ¼ cup lemon juice
- A pinch of lemon zest, grated

### DIRECTIONS:
- In your food processor, mix the bananas with the rest of the ingredients, pulse well, and spread on the bottom of a pan greased with a drizzle of oil.
- Introduce it in the fridge for 30 minutes, slice it into squares and serve.

Nutrition: Calories 136g Fat 11. 2g Carbs 7g Protein 1. 1g

## Black Tea Cake

**PREPARATION TIME: 10 MINUTES**
**COOKING TIME: 35 MINUTES**
**SERVINGS: 8**

### INGREDIENTS:
- tbsp. black tea powder
- cups almond milk, warmed up
- 1 cup avocado oil
- cups stevia
- eggs
- tsp. vanilla extract
- and ½ cups almond flour
- 1 tsp. baking soda
- tsp. baking powder

### DIRECTIONS:
- In a bowl, combine the almond milk with the oil, stevia, and the rest of the ingredients and whisk well.
- Pour this into a cake pan lined with parchment paper, introduce it into the oven at 350°F and bake for 35 minutes.
- Leave the cake to cool down, slice, and serve.

Nutrition: Calories 200 Fat 6. 4g Carbs 6. 5g Protein 5. 4g

## Strawberries Cream

**PREPARATION TIME: 10 MINUTES**
**COOKING TIME: 20 MINUTES**
**SERVINGS: 4**

### INGREDIENTS:
- ½ cup stevia
- lb. strawberries, chopped
- 1 cup almond milk
- Zest of 1 lemon, grated
- ½ cup heavy cream
- egg yolks, whisked

### DIRECTIONS:
- Heat up a pan with the milk over medium-high heat, add the stevia and the rest of the ingredients, whisk well, simmer for 20 minutes, divide into cups and serve cold.

Nutrition: Calories 152 Fat 4. 4g Carbs 5. 1g Protein 0. 8g

## Cinnamon Chickpeas Cookies

**PREPARATION TIME: 10 MINUTES**
**COOKING TIME: 20 MINUTES**
**SERVINGS: 12**

### INGREDIENTS:
- 1 cup canned chickpeas, drained, rinsed, and mashed
- cups almond flour
- 1 tsp. cinnamon powder
- 1 tsp. baking powder
- 1 cup avocado oil
- ½ cup stevia
- 1 egg, whisked
- tsp. almond extract
- 1 cup raisins
- 1 cup coconut, unsweetened and shredded

### DIRECTIONS:
- In a bowl, combine the chickpeas with the flour, cinnamon, and the other ingredients, and whisk well until you obtain a dough.
- Scoop tbsp. of dough on a baking sheet lined with parchment paper, introduce them to the oven at 350°F, and bake for 20 minutes.
- Leave them to cool down for a few minutes and serve.

Nutrition: Calories 200 Fat 4. 5g Carbs 9. 5g Protein 2. 4g

## Cocoa Brownies

**PREPARATION TIME: 10 MINUTES**
**COOKING TIME: 20 MINUTES**
**SERVINGS: 8**

### INGREDIENTS:
- 30 oz. canned lentils, rinsed and drained
- 1 tbsp. honey
- 1 banana, peeled and chopped
- ½ tsp. baking soda
- tbsp. almond butter
- tbsp. cocoa powder
- Cooking spray

### DIRECTIONS:
- In a food processor, combine the lentils with the honey and the other ingredients except for the cooking spray and pulse well.
- Pour this into a pan greased with cooking spray, spread evenly, introduce it to the oven at 375°F and bake for 20 minutes.
- Cut the brownies and serve cold.

Nutrition: Calories 200 Fat 4. 5g Carbs 8. 7g Protein 4. 3g

## Cardamom Almond Cream

**PREPARATION TIME: 30 MINUTES**
**COOKING TIME: 0 MINUTES**
**SERVINGS: 4**

### INGREDIENTS:
- Juice of 1 lime
- ½ cup stevia
- 1 and ½ cups of water
- cups almond milk
- ½ cup honey
- tsp. cardamom, ground
- 1 tsp. rose water
- 1 tsp. vanilla extract

### DIRECTIONS:
- In a blender, combine the almond milk with the cardamom and the rest of the ingredients, pulse well, divide into cups and keep in the fridge for 30 minutes before serving.

Nutrition: Calories 283  Fat 11. 8g  Carbs 4. 7g  Protein 7. 1g

## Banana Cinnamon Cupcakes

**PREPARATION TIME: 10 MINUTES**
**COOKING TIME: 20 MINUTES**
**SERVINGS: 4**

### INGREDIENTS:
- tbsp. avocado oil
- eggs
- ½ cup orange juice
- tsp. cinnamon powder
- 1 tsp. vanilla extract
- bananas, peeled and chopped
- ¾ cup almond flour
- ½ tsp. baking powder
- Cooking spray

### DIRECTIONS:
- In a bowl, combine the oil with the eggs, orange juice, and the other ingredients except for the cooking spray, whisk well, pour into a cupcake pan greased with the cooking spray, and introduce in the oven at 350°F and bake for 20 minutes.
- Cool the cupcakes down and serve.

Nutrition: Calories 142 Fat 5. 8g Carbs 5. 7g Protein 1. 6g

## Rhubarb and Apple Cream

**PREPARATION TIME:** 10 MINUTES
**COOKING TIME:** 0 MINUTES
**SERVINGS:** 6

### INGREDIENTS:
- cups rhubarb, chopped
- 1 and ½ cups stevia
- eggs, whisked
- ½ tsp. nutmeg, ground
- 1 tbsp. avocado oil
- 1/3 cup almond milk

### DIRECTIONS:
- In a blender, combine the rhubarb with the stevia and the rest of the ingredients, pulse well, divide into cups and serve cold.

Nutrition: Calories 200 Fat 5. 2g Carbs 7. 6g Protein 2. 5g

## Almond Rice Dessert

**PREPARATION TIME:** 10 MINUTES
**COOKING TIME:** 20 MINUTES
**SERVINGS:** 4

### INGREDIENTS:
- 1 cup white rice
- cups almond milk
- 1 cup almonds, chopped
- ½ cup stevia
- 1 tbsp. cinnamon powder
- ½ cup pomegranate seeds

### DIRECTIONS:
- In a pot, mix the rice with the milk and stevia, bring to a simmer and cook for 20 minutes, stirring often.
- Add the rest of the ingredients, stir, divide into bowls and serve.

Nutrition: Calories 234 Fat 9. 5g Carbs 12. 4g Protein 6. 5g

## Blueberries Stew

**PREPARATION TIME: 10 MINUTES**
**COOKING TIME: 10 MINUTES**
**SERVINGS: 4**

### INGREDIENTS:
- cups blueberries
- tbsp. stevia
- 1 and ½ cups pure apple juice
- 1 tsp. vanilla extract

### DIRECTIONS:
- In a pan, combine the blueberries with stevia and the other ingredients, bring to a simmer and cook over medium-low heat for 10 minutes.
- Divide into cups and serve cold.

Nutrition: Calories 192 Fat 5. 4g Carbs 9. 4g Protein 4. 5g

## Mandarin Cream

**PREPARATION TIME: 20 MINUTES**
**COOKING TIME: 0 MINUTES**
**SERVINGS: 8**

### INGREDIENTS:
- mandarins, peeled and cut into segments
- Juice of 2 mandarins
- tbsp. stevia
- eggs, whisked
- ¾ cup stevia
- ¾ cup almonds, ground

### DIRECTIONS:
- In a blender, combine the mandarins with the mandarin's juice and the other ingredients, whisk well, divide into cups and keep in the fridge for 20 minutes before serving.

Nutrition: Calories 106 Fat 3. 4g Carbs 2. 4g Protein 4g

## Creamy Mint Strawberry Mix

**PREPARATION TIME:** 10 MINUTES
**COOKING TIME:** 30 MINUTES
**SERVINGS:** 6

### INGREDIENTS:
- Cooking spray
- ¼ cup stevia
- 1 and ½ cup almond flour
- 1 tsp. baking powder
- 1 cup almond milk
- 1 egg, whisked
- cups strawberries, sliced
- 1 tbsp. mint, chopped
- 1 tsp. lime zest, grated
- ½ cup whipping cream

### DIRECTIONS:
- In a bowl, combine the almond with the strawberries, mint, and the other ingredients except for the cooking spray and whisk well.
- Grease 6 ramekins with the cooking spray, pour the strawberry mix inside, introduce it into the oven and bake at 350°F for 30 minutes.
- Cooldown and serve.

Nutrition: Calories 200 Fat 6. 3g Carbs 6. 5g Protein 8g

## Vanilla Cake

**PREPARATION TIME:** 10 MINUTES
**COOKING TIME:** 25 MINUTES
**SERVINGS:** 10

### INGREDIENTS:
- cups almond flour
- tsp. baking powder
- 1 cup olive oil
- 1 and ½ cup almond milk
- 1 and 2/3 cup stevia
- cups water
- 1 tbsp. lime juice
- tsp. vanilla extract
- Cooking spray

### DIRECTIONS:
- In a bowl, mix the almond flour with the baking powder, the oil, and the rest of the ingredients except the cooking spray and whisk well.
- Pour the mix into a cake pan greased with the cooking spray, introduce it into the oven, and bake at 370°F for 25 minutes.
- Leave the cake to cool down, cut, and serve!

Nutrition: Calories 200 Fat 7. 6g Carbs 5. 5g Protein 4. 5g

# Conversion Charts

| VOLUME CONVERSION | | WEIGHT CONVERSION | | TEMPERATURE CONVERSION | |
|---|---|---|---|---|---|
| US | Matric | Ounces | Grams | Fahrenheit | Celsius |
| 1 teaspoon | 5 ml | 1/2 | 14 | 100° | 37° |
| 2 teaspoon | 10 ml | 3/4 | 21 | 150° | 56° |
| 1 tablespoon | 15 ml | 1 | 28 | 200° | 93° |
| 2 tablespoon | 30 ml | 11/2 | 43 | 250° | 121° |
| 1/4 cup | 59 ml | 2 | 57 | 300° | 150° |
| 1/3 cup | 79 ml | 21/2 | 71 | 325° | 160° |
| 1/2 cup | 118 ml | 3 | 85 | 350° | 180° |
| 3/4 cup | 177 ml | 31/2 | 99 | 375° | 190° |
| 1 cup | 237 ml | 4 | 113 | 400° | 200° |
| 11/4 cup | 296 ml | 41/2 | 128 | 425° | 220° |
| 11/2 cup | 355 ml | 5 | 142 | 450° | 230° |
| 13/4 cup | 414 ml | 6 | 170 | 500° | 260° |
| 2 cups (1 pint) | 473 ml | 7 | 198 | 525° | 274° |
| 21/2 cups | 591 ml | 8 | 227 | 550° | 288° |
| 3 cups | 255 | 9 | 255 | | |
| 4 cups (1 quart) | 710 ml | 10 | 283 | | |
| 1.06 quarts | 1 liter | 12 | 340 | | |
| 4 quarts (1 gallon) | 3.8 liter | 16 (1 pound) | 454 | | |

# Recipes Index

## A

Almond Rice Dessert, 9, 12, 13, 32
antioxidants, 5
artificial ingredients, 7
Arugula and Mango, 9, 11, 15, 18
Arugula Walnut Pesto, 11, 12, 13, 18
Asparagus Avocado Soup, 12, 14, 23
Avocado Toast, 25

## B

Bagna Cauda, 11, 13, 14, 18
Baked Black-Eyed Peas, 11, 12, 14, 15, 18
Baked Ricotta & Pears, 13, 18
Banana Cinnamon Cupcakes, 9, 12, 14, 31
Banana Nut Oatmeal, 8, 11, 14, 15, 17, 18
Banana Shake Bowls, 8, 10, 11, 12, 13, 14, 15, 28
Battuto, 7
Belizean Chicken Stew, 14, 22
Black Tea Cake, 10, 11, 12, 15, 29
Blueberries Stew, 9, 12, 13, 33
Braised Chicken with Mushrooms and Olives, 9, 13, 18
Breakfast Couscous, 12, 14, 15, 19, 23, 25
Brown Rice Pilaf with Raisins, 12, 14, 18
Bulgur Salad with Carrots and Almonds, 10, 11, 12, 13, 15, 18, 22

## C

CaFE Cooler, 11, 18
Canned tomatoes, 6
Cannellini Bean Soup, 20
cannellini beans, 6
Cannellini Beans and Farro Stew, 11, 15, 18
Cardamom Almond Cream, 9, 12, 14, 31
carotenoids, 6
Carrot and Bean Stuffed Peppers, 9, 15, 18
Carrot Salad, 11, 18
Cauliflower and Cherry Tomato Salad, 11, 12, 18
Cauliflower Soup, 12, 13, 22
Cauliflower Tabbouleh, 11, 18
Cheesy Stuffed Tomatoes, 11, 12, 14, 15, 19
Chicken and Leeks Pan, 13, 19
Chicken and Peppers Mix, 13, 20
Chicken Shawarma, 9, 11, 18
Chicken Skillet, 9, 12, 13, 14, 18
Chicken Stuffed Peppers, 13, 18
Chicken with Greek, 12, 18
Chicken with Olives, Mustard Greens, and Lemon, 12, 18
Chickpeas, Tomato and Kale Stew, 14, 25
Chilled Pea and mint soup, 19
Cinnamon Chickpeas Cookies, 9, 11, 12, 14, 30
Citrus Salad, 13, 18
Citrus-Kissed Melon, 13, 18
Cocoa Brownies, 9, 11, 12, 13, 14, 30
Coconut Porridge, 13, 14, 15, 18
Cold Lemon Squares, 8, 9, 10, 11, 12, 13, 14, 15, 28
Coriander Falafel, 9, 10, 11, 12, 13, 14, 18, 25, 18
Coronation Chicken Salad Sirtfood, 13, 18
Cream of Thyme Tomato Soup, 19
Creamy broccoli soup, 9, 11, 12, 14, 18
Creamy Cauliflower Soup, 10, 11, 13, 21, 34
Creamy Chicken Soup, 12, 14, 26
Creamy Mint Strawberry Mix, 11, 13, 34
Creamy Panini, 12, 13, 15, 24
Cucumber Soup, 12, 15, 24
Cucumber Yogurt Dip, 11, 12, 18

## D

Dandelion and Strawberry, 11, 12, 18
Date and Walnut, 5, 6, 12, 13, 15, 18
déjà vu moment, 4

## E

Easy Cauliflower Soup, 3, 9, 10, 14, 15
Easy Tzatziki Sauce, 8, 11, 12, 13, 14, 18, 26, 34
Egg, Pancetta, and Spinach Benedict, 11, 17
Eggs and Greens, 12, 13, 18

## F

Fava Beans With Basmati Rice, 11, 12, 18
Fermented yogurt, 6
Freekeh Pilaf, 3, 9, 11, 12, 14, 15, 18
Fresh Tomato Pasta Bowl, 12, 13, 18
Full Eggs in a Squash, 12, 13, 18

## G

Garlic and Lemon Chicken Dish, 21
Garlic Eggplant Slices, 1, 2, 3, 4, 5, 6, 7, 8, 9, 10, 11, 12, 13, 14, 15, 17, 18, 19, 25, 18, 19, 20, 21, 32, 38
Garlicky Broiled Sardines, 12, 13, 18
Garlicky Scrambled Eggs, 26
Gnocchi Ham Olives, 12, 13, 18
Greek Inspired Rice, 11, 13, 18
Green breakfast soup, 11, 18
Guaca Egg Scramble, 8, 11, 18

## H

Harissa Sauce, 12, 13, 18
HDL cholesterol, 4
Heart-Healthful Trail Mix, 11, 18
Herbed Rice, 12, 13, 18
Herbed Risotto, 11, 19
Honey Balsamic Chicken, 13, 20

## I

inflammation, 4

## L

LDL, 5
Lemon Green Beans with Red Onion, 9, 14, 18
Lentils in Tomato Sauce, 13, 18

## M

Mandarin Cream, 9, 12, 13, 33
Marinara Sauce, 12, 13, 18
Mediterranean diet, 4
Mediterranean Eggs, 14, 18
Mediterranean Feta and Quinoa Egg Muffins, 1, 3, 4, 5, 6, 7, 11, 12, 13, 14, 15, 18, 38
Mediterranean Frittata, 13, 14, 15, 26
Mediterranean Spiced Lentils, 11, 12, 18
Mediterranean Spinach and Beans, 9, 11, 13, 14, 15, 18, 20, 18
Mint avocado chilled soup, 10, 13, 21
Minty Lentil and Spinach Soup, 8, 9, 11, 12, 13, 14, 15, 23
Mushroom barley soup, 9, 13, 18
Mushroom soup, 11, 15, 20, 18

## O

Octopus and Radish Salad, 13, 18
Olives and Cheese Stuffed Tomatoes, 12, 13, 18
omega-3 fatty acids, 5

## P

Paprika Chicken Mix, 13, 19
Peach Sunrise Smoothie, 11, 13, 18
Pepper Tapenade, 11, 12, 13, 14, 15, 18
Pineapple Salsa, 12, 13, 18
Pistachio-Crusted Halibut, 14, 22
polyphenols, 6
Potato And Chickpea Hash, 24

## Q

Quinoa, 5
Quinoa, Bean, and Vegetable Stew, 14, 18

## R

Ratatouille, 11, 14, 17, 18
Rhubarb and Apple Cream, 9, 12, 13, 32
Rice and Veggie Jambalaya, 3, 9, 10, 11, 12, 13, 14, 18
Ricotta Stuffed Bell Peppers, 13, 18
Roasted Acorn Squash with Sage, 14, 18
Roasted Asparagus and Tomatoes, 13, 18
Roasted tomato basil soup, 11, 18
Rocket Tomatoes and Mushroom Frittata, 12, 13, 18
Rosemary Garlic, 6, 11, 12, 13, 18

## S

Salmon soup, 6, 11, 18
Savory Avocado Spread, 12, 19
Savory Sweet Potatoes with Parmesan, 11, 13, 14, 15, 18
Shrimp & Arugula Soup, 3, 10, 11, 12, 13, 14
Shrimp Soup, 12, 24
Soaking Beans, 7
Spanakopita Dip, 12, 13, 18
Spicy Early Morning Seafood Risotto, 12, 18
Spinach Cheese Pies, 14, 18
Strawberries Cream, 10, 11, 12, 13, 15, 29
Sweet Potato Tart, 12, 18

## T

Tarragon Grapefruit Dressing, 11, 13, 14, 18
tocopherols, 6
Tomato and Dill Frittata, 11, 13, 18
Tomato and Millet Mix, 11, 12, 13, 14, 19, 18
Tomato Bruschetta, 12, 18
Turkey and Asparagus Mix, 9, 11, 12, 13, 14, 26, 18, 19, 20, 21, 22

## V

Vanilla Cake, 10, 11, 13, 15, 34
Vibrant carrot soup, 9, 11, 12, 13, 18
vitamins, 5

## W

Warm Chicken Avocado Salad, 12, 14, 15, 21

## Y

Yogurt Dip, 12, 13, 14, 15, 18

## Z

Zucchini with Garlic and Red Pepper, 9, 10, 11, 12, 14, 15, 18, 21

# Final Words

In comparison to many other diets, the Mediterranean diet places a larger focus on plant foods. It is not uncommon for whole grains, veggies, and legumes to make up the majority of a meal or a large portion of it. These foods are often made with nutritious fats such as olive oil and a substantial number of fragrant spices. Meals can contain trace amounts of fish, pork, or eggs. sparkling water, water, and plain water are all popular beverages; moderate amounts of red wine are also appropriate.

The best approach to begin transitioning to a Mediterranean diet is to make little adjustments. This can be performed by substituting olive oil for butter when sautéing meals.

- Reduce your consumption of high-fat dairy products by switching to skim milk.
- Opting for whole-wheat bread, pasta, and rice instead of processed grains.
- Increasing vegetable and fruit consumption through salads served as an appetizer or side dish, fruit snacks, and vegetable additions to other recipes.
- At least twice a week, substituting red meat for fish.

According to a study, the Mediterranean diet can improve cholesterol and blood sugar levels, potentially lessening one's risk of developing Alzheimer's disease or dementia. At any age, reducing your risk of developing heart disease or cancer can reduce your risk of dying by 20%. If you are an older adult, the nutrients found in a Mediterranean diet can help you prevent or treat muscle spasms and other indicators of weakness by about 70%.

The Mediterranean diet, when followed as a balanced eating pattern, has been demonstrated to decrease the risk of cardiovascular disease, improve lifespan, and promote good aging. When paired with calorie restriction, the diet can also help you lose weight safely.

In general, a person sahould try a diet that is high in natural foods, such as whole grains, veggies, and healthy fats. Anyone who is dissatisfied with their diet should seek the advice of a nutritionist. They will suggest additional or alternative items that will assist in boosting satiety.

# THANK YOU

Thank you very much for taking time to read this book. I hope it positively impacts your life in ways you can't even imagine.

If you have a minute to spare, I would really appreciate a few words on the site where you bought it.

Honest feedbacks help readers find the right book for their needs!

## Grace Rose

Made in the USA
Columbia, SC
13 August 2022